Introducing

Special Educational Needs

A companion guide for student teachers

PHILIP GARNER AND JOHN DWYFOR DAVIES

David Fulton Publishers
London

David Fulton Publishers Ltd
Ormond House, 26–27 Boswell Street, London WC1N 3JZ

www.fultonpublishers.co.uk

First published in Great Britain by David Fulton Publishers 2001
Reprinted 2001

Note: The right of Philip Garner and John Dwyfor Davies to be identified as the authors of this work has been asserted by them in accordance with the Copyright, Designs and Patents Act 1988.

Copyright © Philip Garner and John Dwyfor Davies 2001

British Library Cataloguing in Publication Data
A catalogue record for this book is available from the British Library

ISBN 1–85346–733–2

The publishers would like to thank Christine Avery for copy-editing and Sophie Cox for proofreading this book

Typeset by Book Production Services, London
Printed in Great Britain by Bell & Bain Ltd, Glasgow

Contents

Acknowledgements

Many individuals have contributed, either unwittingly or more proactively, to this book. We would firstly like to thank the many hundreds of student teachers and newly qualified practitioners for their inputs to our ongoing personal research on the topic of SEN and Teacher Education. Their views concerning the need to provide a more substantial coverage of SEN and inclusion issues during teacher preparation courses have provided the principal motivation for getting this book published.

We would like also to acknowledge feedback from SENCOs, school mentors and others associated with the development of the school-based delivery element of ITT (initial teacher training) courses at both the University of the West of England, Bristol and the Nottingham Trent University. Their inputs have been valuable, as has their continued support. Similarly we extend thanks to numerous colleagues working in local education authorities, whose efforts are so vital in supporting new teachers in schools.

In part this book owes much to the work of Sarah Sandow, formerly Reader in Education at Brunel University. Sarah had the foresight to recognise the growing inadequacies of SEN inputs to ITT courses. Her *Short Guide to Special Educational Needs* was the staple for many undergraduate and PGCE students over many years, and the benefits that student teachers derived from it prompted us to develop the idea further.

Several people have helped us in providing both insights and illustrative material for this book. Penny Barrett, Inclusion Coordinator for Nottingham City Council, and the Education Department of Nottingham City, gave us permission to use examples of draft IEP *proformas* currently being piloted by the LEA. Veronica Lee provided an example of a school's SEN Policy Statement and an example of a SENCO's job description. Mike Parsons, SENCO at Hengrove Primary School, Bristol, gave us details of an LSA's job description. Rob Bowen, Principal Lecturer in Primary Education at the Nottingham Trent University assisted us by providing a number of proformas used in that HEI's undergraduate teacher education courses. Thanks also are owed to Tim O'Brien (Institute of Education, London University) and Dennis Guiney (Educational Psychologist at the Service for Adolescents and Families in Enfield (SAFE) Middlesex) for sharing some of their emerging thoughts on the mysteries of differentiation, target setting and individual education plans.

It is important to acknowledge that the usefulness of this book to student teachers is based in part on the school-based, 'finding out' tasks which complement each of its sections. We therefore offer our thanks, in advance, anticipating the supportive involvement of class teachers, SENCOs, learning support assistants and others currently working in schools.

During our work on this book we have received both moral support and guidance from our publisher. Many student teachers and teachers have benefited from David Fulton Publishers' interest in the field of SEN and inclusion. It is worth recording that our bibliography for this book contains a significant number of Fulton's own publications. This is an indication of their widespread impact.

Finally, thanks are also due to colleagues in our respective institutions, both 'specialist' SEN tutors as well as others engaged in teacher education and those who assist in the administration of such courses. The need for this book in no way represents criticism of their long-standing and continuing efforts to secure an appropriate level of coverage of SEN in teacher education courses. It is an attempt to complement that work in order to contribute to a coherent introductory overview of SEN for trainee teachers.

Glossary of terms

The field of special educational needs, like many other aspects of education, contains a bewildering array of acronyms and abbreviations. Here is a list of the more common ones you will encounter during your training and in your subsequent work as a teacher.

ADHD	Attention Deficit Hyperactivity Disorder
ASD	Autistic Spectrum Disorder
AWCEBD	Association of Workers for Children with Emotional and Behavioural Difficulties
BDA	British Dyslexia Association
BILD	British Institute of Learning Difficulties
BSP	Behaviour Support Plan
CoP	Code of Practice on the Identification and Assessment of Special Educational Needs
CSIE	Centre for Studies in Inclusive Education
DES	Department of Education and Science
DfEE	Department for Education and Employment
DfES	Department for Education and Skills
EBD	Emotional and Behavioural Difficulties
EP	Educational Psychologist
EPS	Educational Psychology Service
ESN(M)	Educationally Sub-normal (moderate)
ESN(S)	Educationally Sub-normal (severe)
EWO	Education Welfare Officer
EWS	Education Welfare Service
HEI	Higher Education Institution
HI	Hearing Impaired
ICT	Information and Communications Technology
IDP	Institutional Development Plan
IEP	Individual Education Plan
INSET	In-Service Education and Training
ITT	Initial Teacher Training
LSA	Learning Support Assistant
LSW	Learning Support Worker

MLD	Moderate Learning Difficulties
NAGSEN	National Advisory Group for Special Educational Needs
NASEN	National Association for Special Educational Needs
NC	National Curriculum
NOF	New Opportunities Fund
NQT	Newly Qualified Teacher
PD	Physical Disability
PMLD	Profound and Multiple Learning Difficulties
PPO	Parent Partnership Officer
PRU	Pupil Referral Unit
PSE	Personal and Social Education
PSP	Pastoral Support Programme
QCA	Qualifications and Curriculum Authority
QTS	Qualified Teacher Status
RNIB	Royal National Institute for the Blind
RNID	Royal National Institute for the Deaf
SEN	Special Educational Needs
SENCO	Special Educational Needs Coordinator
SENTC	Special Educational Needs Training Consortium
SENTAG	Special Educational Needs Training and Advisory Group
SLD	Severe Learning Difficulties
SLT	Speech and Language Therapy
SpLD	Specific Learning Difficulties
TA	Teaching Assistant
VI	Visually Impaired

A note for tutors and school mentors

This book is based on a viewpoint, which we share with many colleagues involved in Initial Teacher Training (ITT) course provision, that inputs regarding special educational needs (SEN) and educational inclusion are frequently marginalised because of the time demand for coverage of subject-specific knowledge and the further erosion of university-based time on account of extended school experience. While acknowledging that both of these are important elements in the development of effective young teachers, it is our belief that a failure to adequately cover SEN during ITT will have a number of negative impacts for newly qualified teachers (NQTs). These will immediately impact on their professional function during their induction period, give rise to increased levels of frustration and stress, and, ultimately, threaten their potential role as key workers in securing more widespread inclusion of children who have learning difficulties in our primary and secondary schools.

We have designed this book to complement, rather than take the place of, formal SEN inputs on ITT courses: much of it is based on an attempt to promote critical reflection on (rather than straightforward information-giving about) SEN matters. Much of the book's content will undoubtedly appear routine and unexceptional to a specialist, experienced SEN tutor or school mentor. Our own research has indicated, however, that many student teachers do not receive such specialist input during their courses. We have therefore sought to provide a basic framework for a study of SEN which can easily be delivered by 'non-specialist' tutors. We have based the content on (i) what might be achievable, given the time pressures facing those who plan, deliver or are recipients of ITT courses and (ii) the themes and issues which both of us regard as comprising the essential knowledge and necessary insights for any new teacher. The content is broadly applicable to students following both undergraduate and postgraduate training programmes, whether primary or secondary in focus. Tutors and school mentors can select specific items (references, questions or tasks) as appropriate to the needs of their own course or situation.

Each chapter of the book comprises:

For students
- easily accessible first-hand information on key SEN themes;
- a set of key questions on each topic;

- a set of key readings for each topic;
- a set of 'school-based tasks' for completion during placements;
- a set of supporting material, including examples, in the appendices.

For tutors/mentors

Each of the above can be adapted by tutors/school mentors for use in formal input sessions. Specifically, though, a set of helpful overhead transparencies for use by tutors/school mentors in these sessions is included in a separate appendix.

The language we have used is straightforward, although a full glossary of SEN-specific terms has been given at the start of the book, because of the proliferation of jargon and acronyms within this area of education.

Each chapter includes sets of easily digestible notes, school-based examples, and summaries using bullet format. We have also made frequent links to web-sites, in order that students can secure first-hand, detailed information regarding specific topics or discussion groups: these are indicated by the motif ▬www▬. A word of caution here, though! Web-sites date very quickly; if any web address we give in this book no longer works the simplest thing to do will be for you to return to any home-page and run a search.

It will be immediately obvious that we have avoided copious reference to the theoretical literature in the body of the book. It is our belief that it is more important to identify and then reinforce a set of core themes and questions in the field, and to do so *without additional references in the text*. You will, however, note that as well as identifying a limited set of references to support each chapter (which can be used as directed reading if necessary) we have provided a substantial bibliography with key texts indicated by an asterisk. As far as our chapter-specific references go, we have tried to restrict our selection to those which students and teachers have told us are especially useful and accessible.

An integral part of the book is the ongoing advice to the student concerning the use of this volume as a focal point for the collection of SEN resources/information. Thus, space is given within the book for students to complete individual school-based tasks, as well as to record their own reflections on a broad range of SEN themes. Finally, a checklist of SEN topics is provided, allowing both student (and the tutor/mentor if appropriate) to assess both extent and depth of coverage and to audit outstanding areas of need.

Throughout the book emphasis is placed on the notion that the volume itself, together with various readings and tasks, represents only a starting point in SEN/inclusive activity. It is also stressed that the key point of reference/discussion for the student is either the university tutor or her school mentor or special educational needs coordinator (SENCO). By drawing on these sources and experiences, together with the judicious use of a carefully selected set of SEN/Inclusive education texts, we hope that this book will not represent a reductionist view of the complexities of the field. Finally, we have attempted to make the text 'talk directly to the student' by adopting an interactive style as far as possible.

(Note: we will refer to 'Initial teacher training' throughout this book because of its widespread official use at the present time; however, we provide opportunities (notably in Part 4) for students/tutors to debate the meanings/ subtleties/distinctions and wider implications of this term and its relationship to teacher 'education' in particular. Moreover, we are anxious to disassociate ourselves from the notion of 'training' as it appears to have been officially adopted by government: teacher education, we believe, is more descriptive of what really takes place on teacher preparation courses – in spite of official controls and directives.)

Introduction

Please take some time to read the following three sections, as they will give you some insights in how best to make use of this book.

1   Why this book?

> By the end of this chapter you should:
>
> • understand the need for this book;
> • recognise the importance of SEN within your ITT programme of study.

During your course of initial teacher training (ITT) you will be required to take account of the needs of children who for one reason or another find it hard to cope in the 'ordinary' classroom and school. It is certainly the case that you will encounter children who present a range of learning difficulties during your school-experience placements or in your formal 'teaching practices'. These children are referred to as having special educational needs (SEN): this term, as you might already be aware, covers a wide range of individual needs, whether physical, social, emotional or intellectual and in many instances combinations of these. In order to meet the needs of these children a complex set of arrangements has, over the last 20 or so years, been established. Much of this, both policy and practice, will have a direct effect on you from the very outset, even though you may only just have started your teacher-training course.

While there is obviously a lot to learn about the whole field of SEN you should not let it become just another aspect of your course which has to be covered. Many teachers will tell you that working with children who have SENs is immensely rewarding. They are right. While you may initially find this aspect of your course quite challenging you will also find that, as you acquire a wider range of skills and as you come to know more about national and regional SEN policy requirements, an invigorating and professionally exciting world will be opened up.

Moreover, it is fair to say that developing your skills and a positive attitude to those children experiencing SEN can have a beneficial effect on your general teaching as well. From a pragmatic point of view, therefore, you will quickly realise that an important contribution to your management of the academic and social learning of a whole class can be made by identifying – and responding to – the individual needs of all pupils. And as you move through your course of initial training you will also become aware that educational inclusion is one of the key policy and practice directions of the twenty-first century. The Green Paper entitled *Excellence for All Children: meeting special educational needs* (DfEE, 1997) stresses that inclusion of all types of learners in schools is one of the major areas for action by

1

central government. It is highly likely therefore, that you will encounter some of the practical issues arising from such practice in both your school experience and in the college-based work on your course.

Major developments are constantly occurring in SEN. In the last few years, ever since the *Code of Practice on the Identification and Assessment of Special Educational Needs* (DFE, 1994), there has been a bewildering number of official publications. These include various planning and guidance documents, as well as government circulars. One of these, the revision of the original Code of Practice, which is effective in schools from January 2002, forms the basis of a major part of this book. Additionally, there have been important advances in the field of professional development and in defining the role of the special educational needs coordinator (SENCO) and specialist teachers for SEN. So there is a lot of information and practical advice to be unearthed in a very short time!

In doing this it is important that you bear in mind that teaching pupils with special needs is not a totally different enterprise from teaching other pupils. Many pupils will present you with a particular challenge, and some of these will be identified as having special educational needs. The current approach to teaching these children, based on equality of access, means that all pupils, irrespective of their stage of intellectual or emotional development, are entitled to experience the full National Curriculum. It will be a major part of your job to provide that access.

In our own work on initial teacher training courses over the last 15 years we have become aware that there has been a problem relating to coverage of SEN within many ITT courses. Tutors involved in such courses frequently state that there is insufficient time to cover important features of SEN, even if they would like to provide more substantial input. This is because so much time has to be spent on dealing with National Curriculum subject knowledge, as well as the fact that students now spend a much greater part of their course in schools than was previously the case – there simply isn't the time available in College to explore SEN matters in greater detail. What we have found, in recent years, is that the quality and depth of student experience in this crucial area of training has been seriously undermined – our research on student opinion regarding this matter shows this clearly.

This book, therefore, is our attempt to do something about this state of affairs. You won't find that it covers everything about SEN (although you will be told where to look for additional information at frequent points) because we are very conscious that, as a busy student teacher, you will probably encounter 'information overload'. So we have been selective in what we have included. In fact, it is fair to say that this book is more about promoting your own thinking about SEN, in order to help dispel some of the myths and create the positive attitudes necessary for young teachers to meet the learning needs of all of their pupils.

Practical task

- In order to begin the process of reflection, write down some of the reasons why you think it is important for student teachers to know more about SEN.

- It might be useful to compare these responses with those of a fellow student teacher.

2 What does this book do?

By the end of this chapter you should:

- understand the core function of this book;
- be familiar with its layout and constituent parts;
- be aware of its core aims.

We are both very conscious of the fact that huge demands are made on student teachers, and that any additional material ought to be concise – while not in any way minimising the great importance of SEN within schools at the present time. When we started planning this book we felt that it was important that we provided a book which, in some ways, enters into a dialogue with you, the student teacher. What we have tried to do, therefore, is to construct a short, easily accessible student 'companion' which is based on a fundamental premise: that new teachers need to become thinkers as well as 'doers'. Hence, while we provide you with some useful references and web-links so that you can find out more, we do not see this book as an 'academic' book. We see it as a student 'companion' which might possibly become the initial collecting point for ideas, reflections and information. Moreover, this book challenges you to think for yourself, so that you can begin to develop a point of view and a personal vision about meeting the SENs of children right from the very outset of your ITT course. So you will find that the book contains lots of questions and lots of self-directed tasks which allow you to make a start on this process.

We have divided the book into four parts. These deal with

- Guiding Principles
- The Revised Code of Practice
- Core Issues for Student Teachers
- Developing Your Future Role.

Each part is divided into a series of sub-sections. In each of these we invite you to explore the material presented from your own developing standpoint as a student teacher. Our coverage of individual 'topics' does not pretend to be exhaustive, but is more directed towards what is 'doable' by you, in the light of all of the other course requirements facing you. *So we will at this point add this note of caution. As we* repeatedly stress, the complexities of SEN and inclusive education make it essential that you make use of the numerous references we provide throughout this book. By doing this and by following the content of each chapter in the book (including the various practical and school-based tasks we have identified) you will have established at least a very good grounding in the subject.

By following the content of this book you will have significantly covered the requirements placed on newly qualified teachers (NQTs) by central government. These state that all newly qualified teachers

> understand their responsibilities as teachers under the SEN Code of Practice and know where and how to get advice from specialists on teaching and learning approaches, and on access strategies for pupils with less commonly occuring types of special educational need.

> (DfES, 2001)

But, just as important, you will have taken the first steps in ensuring that you can make a positive contribution to the exciting development leading towards educational inclusion in our schools.

By the time you reach the end of this book, therefore, you will have achieved, or gone some way towards:

- gaining an understanding of the history of SEN provision;
- exploring your own feelings and initial views in relation to SEN;
- developing an awareness of the current context of SEN provision in schools;
- investigating the nature of SEN in your placement school;
- considering the implications of the latest version of the Code of Practice;
- understanding your role in SEN as a classroom teacher;
- developing an understanding of some basic strategies to meet pupils' SENs;
- gaining an insight into the relationship between misbehaviour and SEN;
- becoming aware of the use and importance of Individual Education Plans (IEPs);
- finding out more about the role of the SENCO;
- becoming familiar with the content of a school's SEN Policy;
- noting the importance of effective relationships with parents/carers;
- exploring some of the 'controversial' issues in SEN;
- beginning the process of mapping your own professional progression relating to SEN.

This checklist will be revisited in the final chapter of this book, in order that you can do a self-audit of your SEN-awareness.

Practical task

Examine the list of potential outcomes of reading this book. Identify TWO of these and briefly explain their importance to you as a student teacher.

Outcome 1_____

Outcome 2 _____

What is the rationale for your choices?

3 Ways of using this book

By the end of this chapter you should:

- be familiar with some of the practical ways in which you can use this book;
- be able to understand the emphasis we place on critically reflecting upon SEN issues.

This book has been designed as a free-standing 'introduction' to SEN, in which you can gradually, over the duration of your teacher-training course, build up a useful set of information and insights. It may also be used as a source of reference both during your ITT course and in your induction year and beyond.

You will note that each chapter provides you with:

- a set of key questions to prompt you to think about the practical considerations raised for you as a new teacher;
- a set of key reference(s) to further inform your thinking and
- a series of school-based 'finding-out' tasks for you to undertake.

One of the things we actively encourage you to do is to make use of your 'companion guide' as a *working notebook* outlining your reflections on SEN policy and practice. Thus, at various points in the book you will encounter a 'task', which invites you to find out about a particular SEN issue in your placement school, or reflect on an aspect of policy or practice. Space is provided for you to record your responses. Used in this way, the book can become a personalised resource or 'portfolio' which you can draw upon as required. It will act as a collecting point for information on SEN you are given during your ITT course, so that you will have this information readily to hand when you need it. You are urged to continue updating your file or 'portfolio' as you move through the initial phase of your teaching career.

In planning this book, we have deliberately placed emphasis upon the importance of your own critical reflections on various aspects of SEN. As with most aspects of general education, we feel that it is important to explore a personal position to support the process of developing an understanding of some of the complex (and often controversial) issues that frequently arise when working with pupils with SEN.

You are also strongly encouraged to refer to the literature mentioned at various points in this book. The references have been selected on the advice of experienced teachers as being particularly accessible and worthwhile. Reading them will help you to gradually build up a body of information and ideas concerning SEN. You will also find that we have identified an extensive set of books in Appendix 1 indicating those which you will find immediately useful. Your tutor/mentor will also have particular suggestions to make.

The use of acronyms, abbreviations and 'jargon' is especially common in SEN. Teachers, other professionals and certainly many SEN publications tend to make frequent use of these, and this can be disconcerting or frustrating to a student teacher, who cannot always draw on the background knowledge of experienced workers in the field. With this in mind we have provided a glossary of the terms you might encounter. We have also tried to keep the use of acronyms to a minimum in this book.

Finally, please note that we use 'he' throughout this book when referring to a child with special needs and 'she' when we make reference to the teacher. This convention curiously reflects the position in many schools with regard to children with learning difficulties: more boys than girls are regarded as having special educational needs, and more women than men are involved in SEN teaching! We have adopted it for the sake of both equity and convenience – but always beware of the many exceptions.

We greatly hope that this companion guide to SEN will be helpful to you in your early years in teaching, both as a student teacher and as an NQT. We welcome any comments or suggestions from you regarding the content – or, indeed, if you wish to discuss aspects of SEN in general! Please contact either of us at our respective institutions. We will be happy to hear from you.

John Dwyfor Davies
University of the West of England, Bristol (john.davies@uwe.ac.uk)

Philip Garner
Nottingham Trent University (philip.garner@ntu.ac.uk)

PART ONE

Guiding Principles

Introduction: what is SEN all about?

Let us begin from the beginning – or, rather, from the standpoint of a common understanding. The first task which needs to be tackled is one of definition – 'Just who exactly are "children with special educational needs"?' SEN is the umbrella term used to describe the wide range of difficulties which prevent children or young people from learning at the rate and level of those children of a similar age. The most recent definition used is that in the *Code of Practice on the Identification and Assessment of Special Educational Needs* (DfEE, 2001).

www http://www.dfee.gov.uk/sen/standard.htm

Thus, a child has *special educational needs* if he has a *learning difficulty* which calls for *special educational provision* to be made for him.
  A child has a *learning difficulty* if he:

(a) has a significantly greater difficulty in learning than the majority of children of the same age; or
(b) has a disability which prevents or hinders the child from making use of educational facilities of a kind generally provided for children of the same age in schools within the area of the local education authority;
(c) is under five and falls within the definition at (a) or (b) above, or would do so if special educational provision was not made for the child.

A child must not be regarded as having a learning difficulty solely because the language or medium of communication of the home is different from the language in which he is or will be taught. *Special educational provision* means:

(a) for a child of two or over, educational provision which is additional to, or otherwise different from, the educational provision made generally for children of the child's age in maintained schools, other than special schools, in the area for a child under two, educational provision of any kind.

(Education Act 1996, Section 312)

The revised version of the Code of Practice now accepts that there are four principal areas of special educational need, relating to:

communication and interaction
cognition and learning
behaviour, emotional and social development
sensory and/or physical.

Each of these is considered in greater detail in Chapter 6 of this book.

As a student teacher you will very soon come into contact with at least some children who fit the description provided above by the DfES. Estimates of precisely how many children in England and Wales have learning difficulties vary, although 'one in five' was an expression coined after the Warnock Report of 1978 to give some indication of numbers. Of this, some 20 per cent, about 2 per cent would have a formal 'statement' of entitlement – a term explained elsewhere in this book.

More recent statistics regarding 'pupils with statements of SEN' show that:

- an estimated 260,500 pupils had statements of SEN in January 2001;
- the percentage of pupils with statements increased from 2.9 per cent in January 1997 to 3.1 per cent in January 2001;
- the percentage of pupils with statements placed in maintained mainstream schools (nursery, primary and secondary) increased from 57.2 per cent in January 1997 to an estimated 61.4 per cent in January 2001;
- the percentage of pupils with statements placed in maintained special schools or pupil referral units (PRUs) decreased from 37.9 per cent in January 1997 to 34.2 per cent in January 2001.

Other statistics regarding pupils with learning difficulties (SEN) without 'statements' show that:

- an estimated 1,554,100 pupils had SEN without statements in January 2001;
- the percentage of pupils with SEN without statements increased from 15.1 per cent in January 1997 to 18.8 per cent in January 2001.

As somebody who is soon to become a classroom teacher, you will have the initial responsibility of meeting the educational needs of such children. Moreover, you are about to enter the teaching profession at a time of exciting developments in SEN. Our thinking has moved now towards a widespread acceptance of the principle of 'inclusive education', in which the way schools are organised and managed, the way in which teachers teach – and the learning opportunities provided for all children – are characterised by flexibility and responsiveness. In this approach children with SEN are the responsibility of all teachers in the school, as well as others (learning support assistants (LSAs), administrators, parent helpers and so on). *No longer are they the sole concern of the member of staff designated as, for example, the SENCO.* It is therefore likely that you will increasingly encounter children whose needs are more severe and complex than hitherto would have been the case in mainstream schools.

Within all of this it is important to remember, however, that the most recent definition of SEN is the culmination of over a hundred years of development. It is highly likely, for instance, that you will have encountered descriptive terms for children who have learning difficulties which are very different in emphasis, as well as some which are not at all positive about the children and young people they are trying to describe!

In this part of the book we begin the process of understanding what exactly is meant by the term SEN, by exploring the recent past, which was characterised by the end to 'categorisation' according to specific handicap. You will have a chance to consider your own views regarding SEN, while Part One also explores some of the main features of current SEN provision and its local and national contexts.

4 Understanding SEN by learning from history

By the end of this chapter you should:

- be aware of the importance of the Warnock Report in the recent development of SEN;
- recognise the key changes in direction that it represented;
- understand the relevance of its recommendations to classroom teachers.

While not minimising the importance of the historical developments that have occurred in 'special' or 'remedial' education (you can explore some of the historical perspectives more fully by reading the key and supportive references to this chapter) we begin our account in 1975, the year when the *Committee of Enquiry into the Education of Handicapped Children and Young People* was established – The Warnock Committee.

'Special educational needs' was the term first coined by the Warnock Committee when it reported its findings in 1978 (DES, 1978). As a starting point we are going to take you back to that time, because it marked a key event in developing a 'new' way of looking at children who had learning difficulties. Its impact is still with us, and so it is important that its findings are fully acknowledged. We regard the Warnock Report, and the 1981 Education Act which was largely based upon it, to be the touchstone of the modern era for SEN provision – indeed, much of what was achieved at that time came to form the basis of the SEN-relevant parts of the 1993 and 1996 Education Acts. At this point it will be useful for you to consider the recent historical development of SEN by examining the timeline presented in Appendix 2. The events indicated in this are included because they are key events in the development of SEN provision, while also enabling you to see 'at a glance', the way in which such provision has rapidly evolved over a relatively short period of time.

It is highly likely that you will read about the work of the Warnock Committee at an early stage of your involvement with SEN. Its deliberations were recorded in the Warnock Report of 1978. For many people this Report represents the start of SEN in its 'modern' idiom, not least because it introduced the term 'special educational needs' itself, to replace terminology which was both outmoded and pejorative to children with learning difficulties. Prior to this time, for example, expressions such as 'backward', 'educationally subnormal' and 'maladjusted' were widely used within education. Warnock adopted a much more positive approach to such children and young people. What is also important is that it heralded the beginning of the more widespread 'integration' of children with SEN into mainstream schools – the forerunner of educational inclusion, a theme you will hear much about on your teacher-training course. The subsequent legislation (The 1981 Education Act) adopted many of Warnock's recommendations (see Appendix 3).

The Warnock Report (1978) identified two groups of children with SEN. The great majority (some 18 per cent of the school population), while experiencing difficulty at some point in their school career, would normally have their needs met within the existing framework of their schools. You will encounter such children as a matter of routine during the initial phases of becoming a qualified teacher. A second, smaller group (some 2 per cent) was also highlighted: these were children whose needs were more serious or complex, and who should be the focus of additional, specialised provision. Thus the Report differentiated between 'recorded' (2 per cent) and 'non-recorded' (18 per cent) special needs in children and young people. This phraseology survives in Scotland to the present day, where reference is made to 'opening a record' and 'maintaining a record', a rather more elegant form than that used in England and Wales (hence Scottish children with this degree of learning difficulty are referred to as 'recorded children'). The 1981 Act used the expression 'a Statement of Special Educational Needs' which gives rise to the now ubiquitous, ugly terms such as 'statemented', 'statementing' and so on.

The main recommendation of the Warnock Committee in respect of children who were 'statemented' was that, in place of ten 'categories of handicap' which had traditionally existed, there should in future be only one definition of special educational need. This would mean that children were no longer to be identified as belonging to one particular group with characteristics in common. The predominant view at the present time is that traditional (pre-Warnock) terminology resulted in the persistence of a 'medicalised' approach to learning difficulties, in which the 'problem' was seen as belonging to the child. This often results in stereotyping and labelling, to the detriment of the educational chances of those children who 'fitted' into each category.

These old 'categories' were clearly formulated in the 1944 Education Act, which identified ten groups of pupils:

- Pupils who are blind
- Pupils who are deaf
- Pupils with partial sight
- Pupils with partial hearing
- Pupils who are termed 'delicate'
- Pupils who have speech defects
- Pupils who are termed 'maladjusted'
- Pupils who have epilepsy
- Pupils who are termed 'educationally subnormal'
- Pupils who have physical handicap.

One of the obvious results of identifying such 'labels' was that it actually helped to create a 'need'. This was typically the case with children who were referred to as being 'maladjusted'. Almost overnight a large group of children assumed this 'label' – followed by the establishment of 'appropriate' provision (usually in the form of a separate special school). A similar situation was to arise later on, during the early 1970s, when another 'category' was created, which identified so-called disruptive pupils, to be followed by a network of 'off-site units' to meet their needs. It is important to note that, before the 'creation' of the title and its attendant provision, such pupils appeared to be mainly catered for in mainstream schools – and without such a negative 'label'.

In contrast to this approach, Warnock recognised that there was in fact a continuum of need from 'very severe' to 'comparatively mild', and that making distinctions between them was arbitrary and harmful. It got in the way of viewing 'educational needs' as multi-dimensional in origin, rather than being the 'fault' of an individual child. The Report also recommended that in place of the 'once-for-all' assessment of handicap, by one professional (usually an educational psychologist), there should be a multi-professional assessment involving psychological, medical and educational reports, together with any others that might be needed. Parents/carers should be able to contribute to the assessment. Importantly the statement of SEN that followed the assessment would then be subject to periodic (annual) review – to which parents/carers were entitled to have input. Warnock made several other proposals about training, research, and about the identification of a 'named person' who was to be a source of information for a family with a child who had special needs.

Take time at this point to have another look at the SEN timeline, contained in Appendix 2.

Key reference

Hermelin, R. (1981) 'A law to last the century', *Special Education: Forward Trends* **8** (4), 6–7.

This article, written in the same year as the Education Act, highlights the weight of expectation that it would lead to an attitudinal change, as well as a commentary on the Act's legal, administrative and philosophical bases.

Supporting references

Bookbinder, G. (1983) 'A new deal or dashed hopes?', *Special Education: Forward Trends* **10** (1), 6–7.
Farrell, P. (2001) 'Special education in the last twenty years: have things really got better?', *British Journal of Special Education* **28** (1), 3–9.
Wedell, K. *et al.* (1982) 'Challenges in the 1981 Act', *Special Education: Forward Trends* **9** (2), 6–8.

Key questions

- Why do you think that Warnock and the 1981 Act are seen as the key events in defining SEN provision at the present time?

- What do you think has been the most lasting effect of Warnock and the 1981 Act?

- What evidence can you give which illustrates that many people still refer to 'categories' of learning difficulty?

School-based task

- Talk to an experienced teacher in your school. What does she recollect about the way in which SEN was organised in her early teaching career?
- Note any similarities and differences between her description and the current situation.

5 Understanding SEN by examining personal views and feelings

By the end of this chapter you should be able to:

- recollect, and reflect on, personal encounters you have had with SEN children;
- think about your own interpretation of the term SEN;
- uncover your responses to disability and SEN.

Much is beginning to be written in educational research concerning the professional 'identity' of the teacher – the way in which the teacher does her job and the values and attitudes which appear to underpin her work. Interest has been directed particularly towards establishing those things which help to contribute to the 'construction' of teacher identity. In general it is assumed that this is formed to a great extent by the teacher's own background, training and experience. We will focus on the first of these in this chapter.

All teachers, and you will certainly be no exception to this, bring to the classroom a set of self-concepts, value systems, likes, dislikes, fears, expectations and so forth. Special education has always been something of an emotive topic, covering some difficult 'territory' and seeming to prompt strong feelings and controversy. Given that this is the case, we believe it is essential that you identify a personal standpoint or position. Put in fairly blunt terms, you need to establish what you stand for when it comes to SEN! A starting point for doing this is by exploring your own viewpoints – you will be able to make a more positive contribution to provision for SEN if you have interrogated yourself.

Consider the following reflective account, for instance. It is written by an experienced teacher, who now recalls her own schooldays:

> As a Girl Guide I remember visiting an institution where there were Down's Syndrome and autistic children. I had to spend two days with them for a badge and it was a real endurance test. I felt very uncomfortable because I had never been with such people. I think I looked down on them as lesser mortals, being thankful that I was not like them. They were outside my

experience and I could not understand how the adults who cared for them could give them so much affection. Even as a Cadet Guider, when a girl with MS joined us I felt she was different and just could not treat her as a normal person. I think that some of my friends were also relieved when she left. I now have two good friends with MS and I know a dear boy with cerebral palsy. I think it is ignorance which breeds fear.

(Garner *et al.* 1995, p. 12)

To what extent do you feel that the sentiments of the writer reveal something about her attitude to SENs? Is it fair to say that fear is bred from ignorance in respect of disabilities? Looking back on your own time as a pupil in school, do you recollect any similar experiences?

It is frequently the case that when certain people meet a disabled child or young person (especially if this is immediately obvious, for instance because of a visible disability) they can feel a sense of awkwardness in not knowing how to interact or respond. This might in part be due to the fact that a personal 'position' has not yet been developed by working through their own feelings about disability and 'difference'.

Some commentators have argued that one of the reasons at the heart of our response to 'difference' – which is often ambiguous or contradictory – is that we are sometimes confused by the 'meaning' of disability. An illustration of this can be found in Johnstone's observation that disabled people are 'either pathetic victims, arch villains or heroes. The stereotype of the disabled child is either that of the brave little lost boy/girl overcoming personal tragedy, or of the scheming malcontent determined to have revenge on society for the misfortune that has befallen him/her' (Johnstone, 1995, pp. 4–5). Put in terms of a child who has an SEN, teachers can feel both a sense of commitment to meeting his educational needs while, on other occasions, feeling somewhat threatened by the 'challenge' which the child presents.

When considering 'difference' – whether physical disability, or learning difficulty, it is often the case that we can slip easily into negative stereotyping. Hence, our view of what SEN means to us at this early stage in our development as a teacher can become polarised between views of children as 'able bodied' (positive) versus 'disabled' (negative), an illustration of which is provided below:

Able bodied	Disabled
Normal	Abnormal
Independent	Dependent
Good	Bad
Clean	Unclean
Fit	Unfit

While the polarities exemplified above are possibly extreme cases, there is no doubt that most teachers tend to develop a 'preferred' type of pupil – in respect of the way in which he approaches learning, his behaviour and so on. However, from this quite natural and understandable position it is only a very short step to negative labelling. Looked at from the standpoint of a classroom teacher, this kind of stereotyping can have serious consequences for the learner.

A further means of gaining an insight into this issue is by considering the range of names – mostly pejorative – which children in school use to characterise or describe others. Children who wear glasses, or who are overweight, children who appear to behave or learn in ways which are unusual, can all be subject to name-calling. A good example of this is the way that children whose behaviour in school is sometimes problematic may be described by a wide variety of unacceptable and stigmatising terms. These may range from 'nutters', 'mad' or 'mental' through to apparently more technical – though no less unsatisfactory – words such as 'disruptive' or 'pupils with problems'. It is entirely possible, too, that you may have heard such expressions being used by adults in other settings, so deep seated is the fear of 'difference' in some people.

Key reference

Norwich, B. (1999) 'The connotations of special education labels for professionals in the field', *British Journal of Special Education* **26** (4), 179–83.

Labelling individuals or groups of children has an important impact on professional attitudes – and influences both provision and teaching in SEN. Brahm Norwich gives details of his research on the attitudes of experienced teachers, trainee teachers and educational psychologists.

Supporting references

Wearmouth, J. (1999) 'Another one flew over: "maladjusted" Jack's perception of his label', *British Journal of Special Education* **26** (1), 15–22.
Garner, P. *et al.* (1995) 'What teachers think', in Garner, P. *et al. What Teachers Do.* London: Paul Chapman Publishing, 3–9.
Brownlee, J. and Carrington, S. (2000) 'Opportunities for authentic experience: a teaching programme designed to change attitudes towards disability for pre-service teachers', *Support for Learning* **15** (3), 99–105.

Key questions

- What do you recollect about SEN from your own childhood/schooling? Do any images stand out?

- Can you recall any of the terms/expressions which you have come across in respect of SEN? Why do you think they are (mainly) pejorative?

- What thoughts/feelings do you have when you meet a person who has a disability?

School-based task

What do some of the teachers you meet in school remember about the terms used to describe children with learning difficulties when they started teaching?

6 Understanding SEN by considering its current context

By the end of this chapter you will have:

- reviewed the characteristics of four groups of SEN as defined in the Code;
- reviewed some of the defining elements of national SEN provision at the present time;
- understood the underlying principles of the new Code of Practice;
- identified the key factors in effective SEN provision in schools;
- recognised that the Code is principally a document of guidance to be used flexibly.

An overview of national provision for children with SEN

In 1998 the DfEE published *Meeting Special Educational Needs. A programme of action.*

www **http://www.dfee.gov.uk/senap/index.htm.**

This working document was developed from the broad principles set out in a Green Paper, *Excellence for All Children: meeting special educational needs* (DfEE, 1997). While the *programme of action* is important in its own right, it is also useful in that it helps us to delineate the key policy themes in SEN at the present time, as well as some of their practical outcomes. Moreover, the document clearly illustrates just how far we have come in our thinking and practice concerning SEN in schools since the period immediately before the Warnock Report.

The Programme of Action is framed around five broad areas of activity:

- working with parents/carers;
- improving the SEN framework;
- developing a more inclusive system;
- developing knowledge and skills;
- working in partnership to meet SENs.

Each of these has an important impact on how you will function as a teacher in respect of children who have learning difficulties. We will now deal briefly with each area of activity, highlighting as we do the implications for you as someone who will, in a very short space of time, be working on a full-time basis in schools. You will perhaps note as we do so that many of the issues covered elsewhere in this book are, in fact, core elements in the Programme of Action.

What is the range of SENs in mainstream schools?

As we have seen, children who have SEN fall into two broad groups: those with severe and complex needs and those whose difficulties are either less severe or not as pervasive. Those relating to the former are frequently (though not always) related to sensory, physical and cognitive impairments, as well as medical/psychological conditions, which are often identified prior to a child starting school or in the early years of formal schooling, and for which the child has a 'statement'. The latter group is more frequently related to matters of general underachievement by a child in one or several curriculum areas, or behaviour which is regarded as unacceptable by his teachers.

The educational needs of both groups cannot be seen in isolation, however. Factors relating to gender, personality, home background, school organisation and so on can all have an impact on the extent to which children experience learning difficulties in the classroom. It is therefore important that you consider the whole child, and not just the SEN as it manifests itself.

It is also crucial that you recognise that many of the 'needs' of these children overlap: a child who exhibits some form of unwanted behaviour over an extended period of time can frequently be underachieving in one or more curriculum areas.

The new Code of Practice, which is part of the Programme of Action and which we explore in greater detail later in this book, refers to four main groups of SEN, which encompass the full range of learning needs, from 'severe' to comparatively 'mild'.

www **http://www.dfee.gov.uk/sen/standard.htm** (para. 7.15 onwards).

At this point it is worth noting that, according to the most recent version of the Code of Practice, children who are referred to as 'very able' are not specifically covered by it – nor should they be on a school's 'register' of SEN.

What the Code of Practice tells us about SENs relating to communication and interaction

Most children with SEN have difficulties in one, some or all of the areas of speech, language and communication. Their communication needs may be both diverse and complex. Moreover, they can manifest these difficulties consistently over time or in particular settings or parts of the curriculum. The range of difficulties covered by this group includes children and young people with speech and language difficulties, specific learning difficulties (including dyslexia and dyspraxia) and hearing impairments. This group would also include children who demonstrate features within the autistic spectrum – including Asperger's Syndrome. Children with moderate, severe or profound learning difficulties (MLD, SLD, PMLD) will almost certainly be included in this grouping.

What the Code of Practice tells us about SENs relating to cognition and learning

Included in this group are children who demonstrate features of moderate, severe or profound learning difficulties or specific learning difficulties (SpLD), such as dyslexia or dyspraxia, and require specific programmes to aid progress in cognition and learning. Such requirements may also apply to some extent to children with physical and sensory impairments and those on the autistic spectrum. Some of these children may have associated sensory, physical and behavioural difficulties that compound their needs.

What the Code of Practice tells us about SENs relating to unacceptable behaviour, emotional and social development

This grouping includes children who demonstrate features of emotional and behavioural difficulties (EBD), who may present withdrawn, depressed or isolated behaviour, or (alternatively) disruptive and challenging behaviours (for example, self-injurious behaviour). This group may also include children who appear hyperactive and lacking in concentration, as well as those with immature social skills. Some children will also present challenging behaviours arising from other complex special needs and may require individual, specialised support or counselling.

What the Code of Practice tells us about SENs relating to sensory and/or physical needs

SEN covers a wide range of sensory, multi-sensory and physical difficulties. Notably, the sensory range extends along a continuum from profound and permanent deafness or visual impairment through to lesser levels of loss, which may only be temporary. Physical impairments may arise from a range of causes. Some physical difficulties require adaptations to existing buildings or resources in order to secure full access to the academic and social curriculum. Those which are more complex include multi-sensory difficulties.

Key elements of the Programme of Action

Let us now return to the Programme of Action and its five areas of activity, all of which are directed towards raising the effectiveness levels of provision for children and young people with SENs.

Working with parents/carers

- An emphasis on earlier identification of SEN means that you will be more likely to encounter children who have already received some input regarding their SEN. It is inevitable that parents/carers will have had considerable involvement, so you should ensure that the positive features of these efforts are built on in your own work with the child. Liaison with parents/carers should be consistent, positive and based on the establishment of mutual trust.
- The establishment of LEA parent partnership schemes should mean an increasing level of parents'/carers' involvement in their child's education. Try to present yourself as someone who is approachable. Talk with parents/carers in a non-threatening way (e.g. do not use unnecessary educational jargon). It is worth bearing in mind that some parents/carers of children with SEN will themselves have had negative experiences as pupils in school.
- Children with SEN should be more involved in the SEN process – from their input into the assessment process, to curriculum strategies, IEPs, behaviour management approaches and so on. You must be very questioning of your own approach in each of these areas – always look for new ways of involving the child who has an SEN (and his parents/carers). And don't forget – the Code of Practice is very explicit about this; in fact, the whole of Chapter 3 of the draft is devoted to this. **www** **http://www.dfee.gov.uk/sen/standard.htm**

Improving the SEN framework

Many of the themes identified in this section of the Programme of Action are covered elsewhere in this book (see chapters 8, 9, 10 and 11). Nevertheless a brief study of what is contained in the Programme will serve as a reminder to you of the vast range of initiatives already underway. In particular, the Revised Code of Practice – a core element of this book – forms an integral component of the enhancement of the SEN framework. While the specific content of the Code as it impacts on a classroom teacher is the subject of the second part of this book, we will at this stage begin by making reference to some of the core principles underpinning the new Code.

The revision of the original Code of Practice (DFE, 1994) is one of the most important elements of the Programme of Action, in order to enhance existing SEN framework of provision. The new Code of Practice has identified five guiding principles which should underpin your thinking and practice in meeting the needs of what is, in many schools, a significant number of children. These principles are equally important to you whether you are a student teacher or a fully qualified and experienced practitioner.

- A child with special educational needs should have his needs met.
- The special educational needs of children will normally be met in mainstream schools or settings.
- The views of the child should be sought and taken into account.
- Parents/carers have a vital role to play in supporting their child's education.
- Children with special educational needs should be offered full access to a broad,

balanced and relevant education, including the Foundation Stage Curriculum and the National Curriculum.

The Revised Code also identifies what are seen as the critical factors in successfully meeting the educational needs of such children. These include:

- that the culture, practice, management and deployment of resources in schools or settings should be designed to ensure all children's needs are met;
- that LEAs, schools and settings should work together to ensure that any child's special educational needs are identified early;
- that LEAs, schools and settings should exploit good and best practice when devising interventions;
- that those responsible for special educational provision should take into account the wishes of the child concerned, in the light of his age and understanding;
- that special education professionals work in partnership with parents/carers and take into account the views of individual parents/carers in respect of their child's particular needs;
- that interventions for each child are reviewed regularly to assess their impact, the child's progress and the views of the child, his teachers and his parents/carers;
- that there is close cooperation between all the agencies concerned and a multi-disciplinary approach to the resolution of issues.

It is very important to recognise that the Code of Practice is essentially a 'guidance' document. What it contains is a series of recommendations for good practice which should be followed on the basis of local needs and contexts. This flexibility is important, in that it allows those who know the children best (the individual school and its teachers) to arrive at the most appropriate SEN strategy for them. But the Code does advise the adoption of

> a strategy that recognises the various levels and complexities of need, the different responsibilities to assess and meet those needs, and the associated range and variations in provision, which will best reflect and promote common recognition of the continuum of special educational needs.
>
> (DfEE, 2001, p.3)

There are also some important legal requirements for provision – these are spelt out in the revised Education (Special Educational Needs) Regulations attached to the new Code. ▪www▪ **http://www.dfee.gov.uk/sen/standard.htm**

Developing a more inclusive system

- As the Programme of Action requires each local education authority (LEA) to establish a policy on inclusion within its overall education development plan (EDP), it is likely that you will encounter some of the strategies resulting from this. Make a point of finding out about this policy both in your placement school and (especially) in your first appointment.

- The Programme of Action provides a range of resources to support inclusion. You will need to be alert to any new additions to your school's resources, as well as keeping an eye out for any training opportunities connected with them. As resources also refers to human resources, you will need to recognise that, both as a student teacher and as an NQT, you are likely to come in contact with many other adults in your classroom (especially Teaching Assistants (TAs) as they are now commonly referred to and parent helpers).
- It is now a statutory requirement that mainstream schools should not discriminate in their admissions policy in respect of SEN. Quite apart from the move towards a more 'inclusive' philosophy in education, this is going to mean the strong likelihood of you meeting an increased range of SENs in your class – including some which are referred to as 'low-incidence' SENs (for example, children with visual or hearing impairments).
- The role of special schools has been highlighted in the Programme of Action. You should be aware of the possibilities of collaboration with teachers working in special schools – in terms of curriculum planning, target setting, pro-social behaviour programmes and so on. Start by finding out the location of special schools in your area, and what specific SENs they cater for. If possible try to arrange a visit – you will probably be very surprised at what you see!
- The Programme of Action places a particular emphasis on improving the arrangements for children who are deemed to have emotional and/or behavioural difficulties (EBD). This group of SEN youngsters, and their educational provision, constitutes one of the most controversial issues in schools at the present time.
  www **http://www.dfee.gov.uk/circulars/dfeepub/jul00/020700/threshold/page6.htm**
  The phrase is indeterminate and is subject to huge variation from school to school, teacher to teacher and from LEA to LEA (see chapter 14 of this book). But this is a significant SEN, in terms of its overall population in mainstream schools. Use this section of the Programme of Action to review the behaviour/discipline policy of your placement school, as well as trying to gather information on an LEA 'behaviour support plan' (BSP) – the formulation of which is a statutory requirement of all LEAs.
  www **http://www.dfee.gov.uk/circulars/1_98/contents.htm**

Developing knowledge and skills

- The Programme of Action places considerable emphasis on a need for *all* teachers to acquire a set of basic skills and understanding about SEN. This should not come as a surprise to you, because educational inclusion is the over-arching imperative of the Programme of Action. You have taken the first steps in securing some of these skills – but make a commitment to ensuring that you keep up-to-date with what is going on in SEN by regularly talking to key teachers in your school(s) and by glancing at the various SEN journals and periodicals from time to time.
- The Programme of Action also recognises the need for some teachers to develop an extended repertoire of skills in order to help meet a range of more complex SEN. These are now contained in the *National Special Educational Needs Specialist*

Standards (TTA, 1999). While there is no immediate need for you to know the detail of these, it may be useful to see what the 'standards' comprise; they also might offer you insights into the work of any specialist teachers that you might come in contact   with.

   `www` **http://www.canteach.gov.uk/info/library/nat_stand.pdf**

- The role of learning support assistants (LSAs) has gradually been extended over the last few years and the Programme of Action provides further guidance for them – as well as the classroom teachers who work with them. LSAs are an immensely valuable resource and will be a source of great support to you in your teaching career. You therefore need to find out more about their role and the ways in which you can best work collaboratively with them.

   `www` **http://www.inclusive.co.uk/greenpap/lsas.shtml**

- The Programme of Action included a commitment to reviewing the role of the educational psychologist (EP). It is likely, for instance, that in your work as a classroom teacher you will have some dealings with EPs. Familiarise yourself with the type of work they will be expected to do by referring to:

   `www` **http://www.dfee.gov.uk/sen/epwg/index.htm**

Working in partnership to meet SENs

- Regional coordination of SEN is emphasised in the Programme of Action. England now has 11 regional SEN partnerships, which work across a range of LEAs on pre-determined activities. These are especially geared to sharing expertise across a wide range of SEN activity. Make sure you obtain contact details for the SEN Partnership in your region.

   `www` **http://www.dfee.gov.uk/sen/regional/index.htm**

- Improved multi-agency working is also sought in the 'programme' – this means more likelihood of you coming into contact with a range of other professionals during the course of your work as a classroom teacher. The list is a very long one: educational psychologists, social workers, probation officers, physiotherapists, speech therapists, psychiatrists, occupational therapists. Try to build up a profile of what each of these important jobs involves. That way you will be better placed to collaborate effectively with them when the occasion arises.

Key reference

Farrell, M. (2000) 'Educational inclusion and raising standards', *British Journal of Special Education* **27** (1), 35–8.

Michael Farrell discusses the Code of Practice, the Green Paper and the Programme of Action in the wider context of educational inclusion. He maps out some of the tensions and opportunities surrounding these initiatives.

Supporting references

Booker, R. (1998) 'Descriptors of special educational need: Arguments for a national framework', *Support for Learning* **13** (1), 9–13.

Porter, J. and Miller, C. (2000) 'Meeting the standards?', *British Journal of Special Education* **27** (2), 72–5.

Simmons, K. (1998) 'Rights at Risk: a response to the Green Paper', *British Journal of Special Education* **25** (1), 9–12.

Key questions

- To what extent do you think that the descriptions of the range of SENs provided by the new Code are more (or less) helpful than what has gone before?

- If you had to prioritise just *one* of the actions in the Programme of Action in helping to meet the SENs of pupils, which one would it be? Give some reasons for your answer.

- Which of the actions contained in the document is likely to be of most impact on you as a new teacher? Again, give some reasons for your answer.

School-based task

Looking at that part of the SEN 'timeline' from 1994 onwards (Appendix 2), choose one event which you consider to be the most influential for SEN practice. What is the reason for your choice? Do teachers in your placement school agree?

7 Understanding SEN by looking at your work in the classroom and the school

By the end of this chapter you will:

* recognise some of the indicators of a range of SENs in your classroom;
* recognise the general role of the class teacher in meeting the needs of all learners;
* reflect on some of the tensions involved in meeting diverse educational needs.

During your ITT course you will become, or have become, very familiar with the National Standards for QTS. These are currently (September 2001) being revised.

www http://www.dfes..gov.uk/consultations/tta/
www http://www.canteach.gov.uk/info/itt/requirements/index.htm

Attention to these will be helpful in establishing the basic requirements, from an official perspective, for the award of qualified teacher status (QTS). But we need to go somewhat further if we are to grasp more fully the importance of developing a positive and, above all, 'thinking' response to the challenges and opportunities of working with children and young people who have learning difficulties. As with other chapters in this book, we do not attempt to be exhaustive in our treatment of a complex topic: all that we provide here are some clues as to how you can get beneath the surface features of the teaching and learning that goes on in your classroom by critically reflecting on the school experiences of youngsters with SEN.

In this chapter, therefore, we take you through some of the key things which you need to be looking for and thinking about, as you develop your own personal vision of the work that you do with children who have different learning needs. Before we move into a consideration of these we would like to reinforce an important underlying principle: all school children are individuals, and all have educational needs. As a teacher you need to move towards developing an understanding that pupils with SEN are part of a continuum of learners. Their needs, though particularised in many cases, should be viewed as points of opportunity for the teacher. Yes, they will present you with a challenge: but your positive response to that challenge will help to foster a classroom ethos which *enables* learners – at whatever level of achievement they have reached.

Identifying need

The process of 'identification' at whatever level is fraught with dangers, and you need to be very clear as to why you are doing it. If the process is overt and public it defeats its object in providing a teacher with information which can then be the source of action. So you need to be watchful that any of the 'identification processes' (teacher observation, case meetings, checklists and so on) do not scapegoat the child – thereby exacerbating the child's difficulties while making your job harder. Identification should have the needs of the child at heart, and should be carried out with respect for the learner. You should also be seeking the advice of a more experienced colleague.

That said, you will obviously be searching for clues which might enable you to find out if a child has a learning difficulty. There are some obvious, common-sense pointers, over and above the standard assessment procedures which individual schools will normally have in place. We have divided these into the four groupings identified in the Revised Code of Practice (DfEE, 2001).

- *Communication and interaction*
  - Poor reading skills
  - Poor memory
  - Difficulties with handwriting
  - Poor hand-eye coordination
  - Oral skills sometimes better than written skills
  - Lack of concentration/poor organising skills
  - Delayed speech and language skills.

- *Cognition and learning*
  - Discrepancy between reading level and age
  - Short attention span
  - Difficulty understanding instructions
  - Reluctance to do written work
  - Incomplete work
  - Off-task behaviours.

- *Behaviour, emotional and social development*
  - Isolated among peer group
  - Last to become a group member
  - Poor attendance/late arrival
  - Plays with younger/older children at break-time
  - Temper tantrums
  - Off-task classroom behaviour (e.g. out of seat, distracting others)
  - Forgetting equipment/homework tasks (e.g. reading)
  - Low self-esteem
  - Tendency to bully/be bullied
  - Always tired
  - General unsocial behaviours.

- *Sensory and/or physical needs*
  - Sometimes ignore instructions
  - Slow to complete tasks
  - Unclear speech
  - Medical conditions
  - Poor fine/gross motor skills.

These can be present in combination, and can be pervasive or episodic (Remember! Many children will have an SEN which, subsequent to teacher intervention, rapidly becomes a thing of the past.) It is equally important to realise that many children will experience difficulties with *some* of the above at *some* time – for a limited period of time. It is when these behaviours become commonplace that you should be alerted. Other difficulties, typically relating to physical needs and to severe and complex SENs, will almost certainly have already been identified at a much earlier stage of the child's development.

Notice, though, that the outline 'list' we have provided says nothing about the child's strengths or aptitudes. It is of the utmost importance that you give some attention to these. In subsequently developing teaching programmes you will need to use these as starting points to enhance the child's learning. So, always ask yourself 'What is this child good at? What does he bring to my classroom that is positive?' In some cases this may be a tough question to respond to; but we are insistent that virtually every child that you come in contact with will have something to contribute to your classroom.

■www■ You can obtain further information regarding each of these areas of SEN by visiting the following pages on the World Wide Web:

http://www.dfee.gov.uk/circulars/dfeepub/jul00/020700/threshold/page4.htm
  (Cognition and learning)
http://www.dfee.gov.uk/circulars/dfeepub/jul00/020700/threshold/page6.htm
  (Emotional and/or behavioural difficulties)
http://www.dfee.gov.uk/circulars/dfeepub/jul00/020700/threshold/page9.htm
  (Sensory/physical needs)
http://www.dfee.gov.uk/circulars/dfeepub/jul00/020700/threshold/page7.htm
  (Communication needs)

What the teacher does

Once a child has been identified as having some kind of learning difficulty he will be placed on the school's 'special needs register'. This allows the SENCO to monitor the range of exceptional needs within her school and provides important basic information to class teachers concerning individual cases. Make sure you find time to discuss its uses with the SENCO in one of your placement schools.

In identifying the 'needs' of children it is important to go on to examine your own teaching approach and classroom organisation. Although both can contribute to meeting the learning needs of children, they can equally become factors in *reinforcing* a child's difficulties. In other words, you have to ask yourself equally searching questions about your own position as you have done about the child. Among the classroom-based issues to explore are:

Do I encourage different types of learning? Which? How?
What do I do to support these?
Do I vary my teaching style? Which? How?
Do I promote flexible, collaborative learning? What range?
Do I plan my classroom with me or the children in mind? (What is your evidence?)
Are my structures clear and unambiguous?
Do I teach all children? (What are your checks?)
Do I give appropriate praise to all children?
Do all children contribute? (How do you know?)
Do I provide alternative means of assessment/success? Which?

Each of these questions (and there are many more, as the *Index for Inclusion* (CSIE, 2000) exhaustively indicates) will provide clues to your own approach to SEN. Ultimately, they are questions which are based on helping to ensure that the concept of 'learning difficulty' becomes more properly located as a consideration of 'learning difference'.

In order to assist you in the process of 'looking at your own practice' we have included, in Appendix 6(i), two *proformas*. The first of these can be used near to the start of your training – to identify some of the approaches you currently adopt in meeting individual needs. This will give you a 'baseline' against which you could assess the ways in which your practice subsequently develops. The second proforma can be used once you have had opportunities to gather more information regarding SEN and inclusion as your course progresses.

We do not minimise the potential problems in attending to a diverse range of learning needs. You will most certainly find this task challenging, and you will need to respond to it with integrity. Above all, you will need to be very honest in dealing with some of the concerns that typically are raised when these issues are considered. Thus, in recent years student teachers have sought to respond to their own questions and viewpoints relating to this, including:

- Won't SEN pupils interfere with my work with the rest of the class?
- Shouldn't SEN pupils be somebody else's responsibility?
- I haven't enough time to prepare separate work for SEN pupils.
- Why should pupils who don't put in the effort get my attention?
- I will be judged on my success in external assessments (SATs/GCSEs) – SEN pupils will threaten my success.
- Won't it be more professionally rewarding to work with pupils who are achieving at a higher level?

Each of these needs to be thought about and debated. What is clear is that experience shows that you will not always be successful in the strategies you use. What we also know, however, is that there are many more 'successes' than 'failures' – and that the pupil with SEN brings to the classroom (and to your teaching) a lot more that is positive than some teachers might realise.

You can obtain further, detailed information on some of the curricular issues arising from these issues by visiting the web-site of the Qualifications and Curriculum Authority (QCA) **www** **http://www.qca.org.uk/ca/5-14/age_related.asp**

Looking at school provision

There are now a great many ways in which the organisation of a school's SEN provision can be reviewed or, as the contemporary fashion would have it, audited. In this section we draw on a composite example of these in order to provide you with two frameworks around which to assess the nature of SEN provision in the whole school. You may wish, at this stage, to refer to the material provided by the Office for Standards in Education (OFSTED), which identifies key inspection issues in both SEN and educational inclusion. **www** **http://www.ofsted.gov.uk/**

One of the ways of looking at SEN provision which we have used successfully with both students and experienced teachers is the 'concept map'. This is, in essence, a graphical account or drawing, of what someone 'sees' when visiting a school or working in it. In the example we provide in Figure 7.1, which is taken from a book about managing SEN in primary schools, a SENCO draws her thoughts about how SEN is organised in her own school. She then gives a brief written account of her 'concept map'. (see Davies *et al.* pp. 27–38)

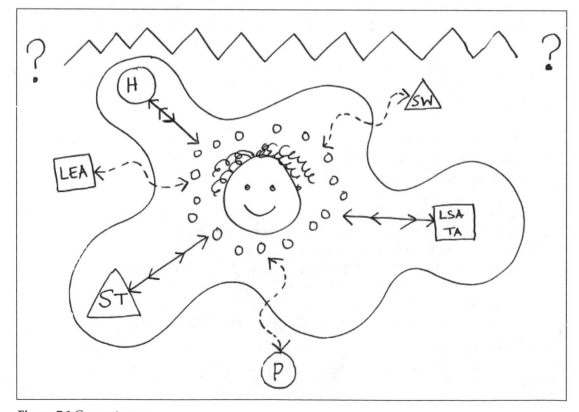

Figure 7.1 Concept map

My name is Helen Royle*, and I am a SENCO in a medium-sized high school in the Midlands. My concept map is easily explained. I'm in the middle (obviously!), surrounded by all of the children who are on the SEN register, at School Action and School Action Plus. They are in this position because they are the most important individuals in my professional life. I have the most contact with three sets of people in the school – the head teacher (H), the subject teachers (STs) and the learning support assistants (LSAs/TAs). Contact is good and direct, hence the straight lines! The school is represented by a wavy line – to show that it is flexible and approachable as far as SEN is concerned. The relationships with parents (P), support workers from the LEA (SW) and the LEA itself (LEA) are all good, but not as direct as those in the school – hence the wavy lines. You'll notice a big jagged line, with a question mark at each end, located menacingly above all of this. It represents the continued pressure I (and the rest of my colleagues, children, parents and others) am under from external forces – league tables, lack of resources, lack of essential skills to manage certain SENs and so on. But generally the picture I have drawn is a positive one. That sums up my work.

* We have changed the author's name, at her own request.

The example provided above offers valuable insights into how its author sees SEN. Equally useful are more formal 'audits', which systematically deal with each aspect of SEN provision. Both examples can be useful in examining one's own position within these processes, as well as providing a vehicle for staff development.

Some of the audit questions (which preferably need to be supported by evidence) are:

- Is the school's SEN policy consistent with official requirements?
- Do all staff seem to be familiar with its content?
- Have all staff been involved in its development?
- Do all staff have access to the SEN register?
- Are the SEN responsibilities of classroom teachers made explicit?
- Do all staff differentiate in their approaches to teaching, learning and resources?
- Do all staff contribute to IEPs?
- Are parents/carers aware of SEN provision?
- Do parents/carers and pupils with SEN help plan their own learning?
- Are LSAs/TAs seen as full members of the school community?
- Are all staff aware of how SEN resources are distributed?
- Is there a policy for staff development in SEN?
- Are staff made aware of visits by external SEN professionals?
- Are frequent opportunities provided to debate SEN/inclusion issues?

You can base your observations about the whole school on the first of the proformas contained in Appendix 10. Use it to evaluate the extent to which the organisational arrangements, systems of communication, classroom arrangements, social climate (or 'ethos') and relationships are supportive of all learners – but especially those who have learning difficulties.

Key reference

Morris, N. and Parker, P. (1997) 'Reviewing the teaching and learning of children with special educational needs: enabling whole school responsibility', *British Journal of Special Education* **24** (4), 163–6.

Supporting references

Bearn, A. and Smith, C. (1998) 'How learning support is perceived by mainstream colleagues', *Support for Learning* **13** (1), 14–20.

Waters, M. (1996) 'Success in the primary classroom: we're all in it together', *Support for Learning* **11** (2), 68–73.

Welding, J. (1996) 'In-class support: A successful way of meeting individual student need', *Support for Learning* **11** (3), 113–17.

Key questions

- Using the checklist provided in this chapter, complete an audit of one school's SEN arrangements.

- What, in your opinion, are the most positive features of your placement school's SEN provision?

- Give an example of how you have recently attempted to meet the exceptional needs of a pupil.

School-based task

Using the guidance provided in this chapter, construct a 'concept map' which summarises your personal view of provision for SEN in your placement school.

PART TWO

The Code of Practice

 Key features and implications

By the end of this chapter you will:

* be familiar with some of the principal elements of the original (1994) Code;
* recognise the main changes introduced in the new Code (2001);
* have assessed the implications of the Code for your work as a teacher.

The *Code of Practice on the Identification and Assessment of Special Educational Needs* was first introduced in 1994. It marked the culmination of a review of SEN arrangements which had existed since the 1981 Education Act, and resulted in some major changes in organisation and management of provision. The Code itself has now been revised, and its impact on schools from the date of its introduction in January 2002 will be widespread.

In its original form the Code set out a framework for SEN policy, practice and provision in six separate sections:

Section 1: Principles and Procedures
Section 2: School-based Stages of Assessment and Provision
Section 3: Statutory Assessment of SEN
Section 4: Statements of SEN
Section 5: Assessment of Under Fives
Section 6: Annual Reviews

We are not going to place heavy emphasis on the original Code of Practice, other than to acknowledge its importance as the Revised Code's predecessor. We deal instead with the latest version, as this will be the one which will have most impact on you both as a student teacher and in your first few years of teaching.

Nevertheless, we do provide, in Appendix 4, an outline of four important elements of the original Code – the 'staged' approach to assessment and intervention, the role of a school's SEN policy, the role of the SENCO, and finally the nature and operation of IEPs. Each of these, in fact, forms the basis of our consideration of the new version of the Code in this part of the book.

Moreover, we also provide, within Appendix 4, some basic information on the process of 'statementing' as it was originally conceptualised in the 1994 Code. It was, and still is, the formal procedure whereby the school, parent/carer, LEA and agencies involved in the health and welfare of the pupil, identify the most appropriate way of meeting the educational needs of that pupil once it becomes clear that additional support is needed. Up-to-date information on what is involved in arriving at a 'statement of SEN' can be obtained by reference to the web.

www **http://www.dfee.gov.uk/sen/standard.htm**

You will have recognised already that the 'revised version' of the Code of Practice is central to the most recent policy initiative on the part of the government – the Programme of Action (see chapter 6 of this book). Following a period of consultation, the Revised Code of Practice saw an important emphasis being placed on the several areas of policy and practice which had been identified by teachers and others as points of concern. In particular it refines further the approaches adopted in the original Code, making them even more responsive to the needs of children while, at the same time, being more accessible and straightforward in layout and language.

The modifications contained in the new Code are intended to:

- develop a more inclusive approach to SEN;
- achieve better cooperation between education, health and social services;
- support looked-after children;
- enhance the role of governing bodies in relation to SEN;
- support children aged under five;
- enhance the links between Early Years and Sure Start initiatives;
- improve the links between exclusions from school and 'education otherwise';
- interface with the National Curriculum and the literacy hour;
- enhance the rights of disabled children to personal support;
- improve conciliation arrangements;
- increase the use of ICT in record keeping;
- address the implications for SEN of the National Childcare Strategy and changes to the NHS;
- comply with the new school framework and the abolition of the Funding Agency for Schools.

The revision takes account of several concerns which were raised by teachers, parents/carers and others following the inception of the original Code of Practice in 1994. We have summarised the key changes that have resulted from the Code's revision elsewhere (see Appendix 5). In this chapter of the book we want to focus on those changes which are likely to have most relevance to you during your ITT course and when you first take up a teaching position in school. We will do this first by making reference to changes in the layout and appearance of the Code but then we will examine four key areas which might impact most on your work in schools.

During the consultation period leading up to the publication of the new Code of Practice much evidence was collated regarding the lack of user-friendliness of the original document. At this point you might wish to seek out a copy of the original version, in order to gauge for yourself the extent to which this was the case. A version of this is likely to be available within your placement school or alternatively, almost certainly in the reference section in your college/university library.

Some of the changes are very utilitarian or cosmetic. For instance, the new version now includes an index at the back of the document – perversely the original included an index which was submerged amidst some supporting technical papers. The Code also makes use of much more colour-coding, enabling teachers and others to locate relevant sections more easily. The widespread use of ICT now requires that the Code is available both as a CD-Rom as well as being available via the DfEE's web-site:

www http://www.dfee.gov.uk/sen/standard.htm

Furthermore, there was a good deal of criticism regarding the inaccessibility of the original Code to non-professionals – and in particular to parents/carers. The revised version uses far less jargon, and it is written in a way which makes it far more meaningful to them – it avoids making the sweeping assumptions that the original Code made about the SEN-specific knowledge base of the reader.

But do not be fooled into thinking that the new Code is simply a collection of cosmetic changes – useful though these amendments are in making the document more widely accessible. Critiques of the original Code, and the consultation on the revision of the Code itself, have prompted some important refinements which are likely to have a significant impact on your work in school. Aspects of these, relating to the role of the classroom teacher, the SENCO, the importance of IEPs and of a school's SEN Policy, are considered in Chapters 9–12 in this part of the book. In this chapter we explore the implications of a 'graduated response' which is central to the new Code.

The Code explicitly highlights the need for flexibility in applying what it refers to as the 'graduated response' to meeting the SENs of children and young people. It promotes the view that the Code is something which ought to be interpreted in the light of the circumstances and context of each individual school. You will already be aware that different schools function in widely different ways, according to their location, the kind of children they work with, the attitudes and experience of teachers, the leadership of the head teacher and so on. So the Code states that 'There is scope for flexibility and variation in the responses adopted by schools, early education settings and LEAs'. From the outset, therefore, it is important to have at the back of your mind such questions as 'What does this mean for me?', or 'Can I do this in a slightly different way?' Responses to these kinds of questions – which you ought to be thinking about from a very early stage – have to bear in mind that the key to the response lies in a further question: 'Will making an adaptation to the Code benefit the child?'

One of the most obvious changes in provision is in what the original Code referred to as the 'stages' of identification and assessment. These have now been reduced from five to just two. They are now termed School Action and School Action Plus and are no longer seen as 'stages' as such.

School Action

A number of triggers for action are identified. As a classroom teacher you will need to be on the look-out for any signs that one of your pupils – in spite of you having provided a differentiated approach to his learning – is still not making progress. Such initial concerns might arise if:

regular talks.

Look out 4 triggers)
copying work
Lol of verbal

- the child fails to respond to targeted approaches in his area of weakness;
- the child is slow to develop age-appropriate literacy/numeracy skills;
- the child presents 'emotional and/or behavioural difficulties' in spite of your use of behaviour management techniques;
- the child has sensory or physical difficulties and fails to make progress in spite of specialist equipment;
- the child has communication/interaction difficulties and makes no progress in spite of your differentiated teaching.

You can acquire further guidance on these 'triggers' by referring to the DfEE publication on SEN 'thresholds'. **www** **http://www.dfee.gov.uk/sen/standard.htm**

An important function of your role within the 'graduated response' is to share your concerns with the parents/carers of the child. This needs to be done sensitively, recognising the natural anxieties that all parents/carers have about their child's progress in school. A new course of action might then be decided upon, which has a very positive effect. But if you still have concerns these must be shared with the SENCO, who might have additional information about the pupil. Before you do this you need to ensure that your 'concerns' are supported by actual 'evidence' – for example, in the form of observation findings, test scores, work record, behaviour monitoring and so forth. The SENCO will be quite correct in demanding this information as the basis for further discussion and action. You should therefore discuss with her what kinds of 'evidence' she will need to take things further. This discussion will also enable you to decide on what kind of additional support you can provide for the child.

From this point it will be the SENCO who takes the lead in any further assessment of the child (although good practice suggests that you will be kept informed of developments). But, as the child's class teacher, you will still retain overall responsibility for the child on a daily basis – and ensure that the planning and delivery of an individualised programme (including the maintenance of IEPs and work records) is carried out effectively. During all of this it is your duty to keep parents/carers informed of any action that is taken. Chapter 9 contains a summary of your responsibilities as a classroom teacher in respect of the Code.

School Action Plus

When it becomes clear that the child is making little progress, in spite of the strategies followed during the 'School Action' period, the external support services will usually be contacted by the SENCO. Support services (mainly from the LEA, but also from the Area Health Authority or Social Services departments) comprise a wide range of professionals who will offer advice to teachers regarding new approaches, but also direct inputs as deemed appropriate. You will probably see, during School Action Plus, the involvement of such people as educational psychologists, speech therapists or literacy consultants. These are typically provided both by the LEA and by outside agencies and according to the Code of Practice should 'advise teachers about new IEPs and fresh targets, provide more specialist assessments, give advice on the use of new or specialist strategies or materials, and in some cases provide support for particular activities'.

The Revised Code of Practice sees the role of these specialists as preventative rather than reactive. It states that:

> Outside specialists can play an important part in the very early identification of special educational needs and in advising schools on effective provision designed to prevent the development of more significant needs. They can act as consultants and be a source for in-service advice on learning and behaviour management strategies for all teachers.

> (p. 100)

So, School Action Plus offers you a genuine opportunity to enhance your own understanding of a particular aspect of SEN by contact with a specialist.

As in the case of School Action, the Code spells out the kinds of 'triggers' that you will need to be alert to. These indicate the need for further, focused action at School Action Plus stage and 'trigger' this when the child:

- continues to fail to respond to targeted approaches in his area of weakness over a long period of time;
- is slow to develop age-appropriate literacy/numeracy skills;
- continues working at National Curriculum levels substantially below that expected of pupils of a similar age;
- presents 'emotional and/or behavioural difficulties' which substantially and regularly interfere with his own learning or that of the class group, in spite of the behaviour management techniques you have attempted;
- has sensory or physical difficulties and requires additional specialist equipment or regular advice or visits from specialist;
- has ongoing communication or interaction difficulties that impede the development of social relationships and cause substantial barriers to learning.

When an external professional is consulted during School Action Plus one of the first things that she will want to see are the child's records, in order to clarify

- which strategies have already been employed and
- which targets have been set and achieved.

It is on the basis of these, and in conversation (particularly) with the child's class teacher, that advice on new and appropriate targets for the child's IEP and on accompanying strategies will be given.

The class teacher, working in partnership with the SENCO, curriculum, literacy and numeracy coordinators and external specialists, and in consultation with parents/carers, will then consider a range of different teaching approaches and appropriate equipment and teaching materials, including the use of ICT. This will result in a new IEP, in which the external specialist will be involved in a variety of ways:

- in an advisory capacity;
- by providing additional specialist assessment;
- by teaching the child directly.

The new IEP for the child will set out fresh teaching and learning strategies for the child and is intended to be implemented, as far as possible, in the normal classroom setting. Responsibility for the delivery of the interventions in the new IEP will remain with the class teacher, thereby further highlighting the pivotal role which she will assume. Further information concerning your involvement with IEPs is contained in Chapter 11.

There may arrive a point at which the classroom teacher, the SENCO and the external professionals, after reviewing the child's performance, decide that the situation has deteriorated. The child still appears not to be making progress, and further action – leading towards a statutory assessment of need – is deemed to be essential. It is at this point that your skill in keeping a full and comprehensive record of the child's learning will reap its rewards.

At the outset of this phase of assessment the LEA will seek evidence from the school that a range of strategies have been attempted over a period of time, and that the success or otherwise of these has been carefully assessed. Clear documentation of the child's SEN and any resulting actions will also be required. And while it is the SENCO who will collate this information it will be the class teacher who will be a principal source of the data. The SEN Thresholds guidance contains useful information regarding the kinds of 'evidence' required to substantiate a particular case. [www] **http://www.dfee.gov.uk/sen/standard.htm**

'Thresholds', it should be explained at this point, have been developed recently in order to provide guidance to help everyone involved in deciding what action to take in response to children's special educational needs – and to enable that provision to be compared with what is being made available for similar children in other schools.

It is important that you bear in mind that each LEA will have its own system of referral, of course. You are advised, at a very early stage, to begin gathering information about how this operates. Do this by asking the SENCO in your school.

To summarise, under School Action Plus a school should be in a position to seek statutory assessment only when it has gathered the following information:

- details of strategies adopted during *School Action* and *School Action Plus*;
- details of individual education plans for the child;
- records of regular reviews of the child's progress;
- the child's attainment levels in National Curriculum areas;
- the child's attainment levels in literacy and numeracy;

- any other assessments of the child (including non-educational);
- the views of the parents/carers and of the child;
- the extent of the involvement of other professionals/agencies;
- the child's medical history where appropriate.

The LEA will then consider whether a statutory assessment is necessary based on this information. In the meantime – and even during any subsequent statutory assessment – the child will continue to be supported through *School Action Plus*. Again, the core function of the class teacher is emphasised.

Key reference

Bowers, T. *et al.* (1998) 'The Code in action: Some school perceptions of its user-friendliness', *Support for Learning* **13** (3), 99–104.

The authors of this paper conclude that, in overall terms, the original Code has been well received by teachers. More teachers in primary, rather than secondary, schools appeared familiar with the Code's contents. The authors identify that workload and bureaucracy, writing IEPs and 'transition planning' were areas of concern, four years after the Code's inception. Their report forms a precursor to the revision of the Code.

Supporting references

Russell, P. (1994) 'The Code of Practice: new partnerships for children with special educational needs', *British Journal of Special Education* **21** (2), 48–52.
Bowers, T. (2000) 'Cold Comfort in the Code', *British Journal of Special Education* **27** (4), 203.
Hornby, G. (1995) 'The Code of Practice: boon or burden?', *British Journal of Special Education* **22** (3), 116–19.

Key questions

- Based on your experiences so far in schools, outline some of the ways the Code of Practice impacts on the daily lives of teachers.

- Identify THREE principal benefits of the Code for the child with SEN.

- Why do you think it is that the Code has created so much discussion among teachers?

School-based task

Talk briefly to three people (a class teacher, a learning support assistant/teaching assistant and a SENCO) about how their work has changed as a result of the Code of Practice. Make brief notes on their responses.

9 The role of the classroom teacher

By the end of this section you will:

- recognise your responsibilities as a classroom teacher under the Code;
- be familiar with some basic strategies to meet a range of SENs;
- be able to identify sources of support and guidance.

The class teacher's responsibilities under the Code of Practice

During your ITT course you will become, or have become, very familiar with the National Standards for QTS – the so-called 'Induction Standards'.

www http://www.canteach.gov.uk/info/itt/requirements/index.htm
www http://www.dfes.gov.uk/consulatations/tta/

Attention to these will be helpful in establishing the basic requirements, from an official perspective, for the award of qualified teacher status (QTS). It should be noted that all of these general requirements have to be taken into consideration in order to meet the individual needs of children. However, one of these is particularly relevant to working with pupils with learning difficulties. It first states that NQTs, when assessed, must, with the help of an experienced teacher where necessary, use assessment to identify and support pupils who are falling behind and/or failing to achieve their potential in learning, or who are experiencing behavioural, emotional and social difficulties.

Moreover, the standards require that teachers are familiar with the Code of Practice on the Identification and Assessment of Special Educational Needs and, as part of their responsibilities under the Code, implement and keep records on individual education plans (IEPs) where applicable.

As you would reasonably expect, the Code of Practice is even more explicit in stating the responsibilities of the classroom teacher. We can summarise these as follows, in the likely sequence that you may encounter them. Note that some actions are indicated as being 'ongoing', implying that these are responsibilities which you will need to fulfil as part of the daily routine of your teaching.

The class teacher and School Action

- The class teacher is responsible for initial identification of a pupil's SEN by (a) observation and (b) continuous assessment.
- The class teacher must develop differentiated approaches to meet identified needs (*ongoing*).
- The class teacher *must* inform the SENCO of any concerns which remain, in spite of the initial attempts to meet the pupil's learning needs.
- The class teacher, working with the SENCO, will decide what help to provide next.
- The class teacher, working with the SENCO, *must* keep the parents/carers informed and (preferably) invite the parents/carers to discuss the concerns and the action taken (*ongoing*).
- The class teacher, working with the SENCO, will help devise an IEP – ensuring inputs from both the parents/carers and the child.
- The class teacher monitors the progress of the child in meeting IEP targets (*ongoing*).
- The class teacher arranges and attends review meetings (with SENCO, parent/carer, and where appropriate, the child).
- The class teacher *must* inform the SENCO of any continuing concerns (*ongoing*).
- The class teacher *must* continue to organise and plan her teaching so that the child's needs are met – including directing the work of LSAs and involving the child in his own IEP monitoring (*ongoing*).

The class teacher and School Action Plus

- The class teacher *must* continue to support the pupil in the ways described in School Action.
- The class teacher should utilise any additional resources or advice as specified by external agencies.
- The class teacher should continue to liaise closely with both SENCO and parents/carers.

In cases where it is decided that, even after exhaustive inputs at both School Action and School Action Plus, a pupil's needs are still not being met, a process of statutory assessment may be initiated (leading to the provision of a Statement of Special Educational Needs). At this stage in your career it is sufficient to say that you need to work closely with your SENCO, who (via the head teacher) will become the principal teacher involved in working with the LEA to develop a statement of need.

Once a statement is issued it becomes the class teacher's responsibility to follow its content. You should always discuss how to proceed at this stage with your SENCO.

As a student teacher, and subsequently as a new classroom teacher, you will be trying to gain as much insight into how children who have learning difficulties actually learn, and what are the factors which either inhibit or promote success for them in school. In order to start this process you need to observe how children learn, and in particular to listen to what they say. Talking with children, in addition, is an excellent way of gaining their trust and confidence. In Appendix 6(ii) we have included some of the strategies you can use to do this.

Some basic classroom strategies to meet a range of SENs

In Chapter 6 you examined four main groupings of SEN, as identified in the Programme of Action. The class teacher can assist in the learning development of these children in numerous ways, many of which are straightforward and could arguably be viewed as representing nothing other than 'good teaching', applicable to all children.

Before turning to these, however, we want first to identify a set of strategies which seem to us to be essential in helping to prevent general underachievement in the curriculum or in social development. Remember that pupils who underachieve cover a broad range: from pupils who are potential high achievers to those who are easily distracted by others. We don't pretend that this is a revolutionary or sophisticated list. Nevertheless, by keeping these strategies at the forefront of her practice the student teacher and the NQT can go some way towards establishing a preventative approach to underachievement. This is a key strategy in ensuring that the level of need does not escalate – it is, essentially, a means of early intervention.

The basic strategies suggested are:

- Plan your lessons!
- Tell your pupils what you want them to achieve by the end of the lesson.
- Include lots of 'signposts' giving pupils an idea of where the learning is taking them.
- Offer pupils a range of small tasks with clear learning targets.
- Keep your instructions clear and short.
- Mix individual and group work.
- Use praise consistently.
- Use differentiation – by input, process and output.
- Make use of summaries.
- Review what has been learnt at the end of the lesson (listen to the pupil!).

In spite of these approaches you may find that some children fail to progress and become a greater cause for concern. It is likely that, after an appropriate period of assessment, such children will be supported at either School Action or School Action Plus. This could be characterised by the following interventions, in each of the four main SEN groupings and which the class teacher can help to support.

Children with SENs relating to communication and interaction

- Flexible teaching arrangements;
- help in acquiring, comprehending and using language;
- help in articulation;
- help in acquiring literacy skills;

– help in using augmentative and alternative means of communication;
– help to use different means of communication confidently and competently for a range of purposes including formal situations;
– help in organising and coordinating oral and written language;
– support to compensate for the impact of a communication difficulty on learning in English as an additional language;
– help in expressing, comprehending and using their own language, where English is not the first language.

Children with SENs relating to cognition and learning

– Flexible teaching arrangements;
– help with processing language, memory and reasoning skills;
– help and support in acquiring literacy skills;
– help in organising and coordinating spoken and written English to aid cognition;
– help with sequencing and organisational skills;
– help with problem solving and developing concepts;
– programmes to aid improvement of fine and motor competencies;
– support in the use of technical terms and abstract ideas;
– help in understanding ideas, concepts and experiences when information cannot be gained through first-hand sensory or physical experiences.

Children with SENs relating to behaviour, emotional and social development

– Flexible teaching arrangements;
– help with development of social competence and emotional maturity;
– help in adjusting to school expectations and routines;
– help in acquiring the skills of positive interaction with peers and adults;
– specialised behavioural and cognitive approaches;
– rechannelling or refocusing to diminish repetitive and self-injurious behaviours;
– provision of class and school systems which control or censure negative or difficult behaviours;
– provision of a safe and supportive environment.

Children with SENs relating to sensory and/or physical needs

– Flexible teaching arrangements;
– appropriate seating, acoustic conditioning and lighting;
– adaptations to the physical environment of the school;
– adaptations to school policies and procedures;
– access to alternative or augmented forms of communication;
– provision of tactile and kinaesthetic materials;
– access to different amplification systems;
– access to low-vision aids;
– access in all areas of the curriculum through specialist aids, equipment or furniture; regular and frequent access to specialist support.

As a student teacher, or as an NQT, there would not be an expectation that you were skilled in all of the strategies listed above: each is a complex process which requires both experience and professional development to refine. Nonetheless, some recognition by you at this stage of what might be possible could be helpful in discussions regarding classroom strategy with the SENCO.

You are advised at this point to cross reference with the information provided in Chapter 7, and particularly to recall your critical reflections on the issues raised as a result of your responses to the questions and school-based task in that chapter. You may also wish to refer to Appendix 6(i) again.

www Finally, reference should again be made to the SEN thresholds, on the following web-sites:

http://www.dfee.gov.uk/circulars/dfeepub/jul00/020700/threshold/page4.htm
(Cognition and learning)
http://www.dfee.gov.uk/circulars/dfeepub/jul00/020700/threshold/page6.htm
(Emotional and/or behavioural difficulties)
http://www.dfee.gov.uk/circulars/dfeepub/jul00/020700/threshold/page9.htm
(Sensory/physical needs)
http://www.dfee.gov.uk/circulars/dfeepub/jul00/020700/threshold/page7.htm
(Communication needs)

Key reference

Gross, J. (2000) 'Paper promises? Making the Code work for you', *Support for Learning* **15** (3), 126–33.

Jean Gross outlines some of the approaches that class teachers can adopt in order to effectively meet individual needs. She is very conscious of the time constraints on teachers, and addresses the issue of bureaucracy. She recommends a targeted aproach in teaching and learning.

Supporting references

Fernandez, M. (2000) 'Educating Mary: a special education case study in one Western Australian high school', *Support for Learning* **15** (3), 118–25.
Banner, G. and Rayner, S. (1997) 'Teaching in style: Are you making the difference in the classroom?', *Support for Learning* **12** (1), 15–18.
Williams, A. (1996) 'Curriculum auditing; an accessible tool or an awesome task?', *British Journal of Special Education* **23** (2), 65–9.

Key questions

- Are the skills required in teaching a child who has an SEN any different to those needed more generally? When do they become different – or 'in addition to'?

- What are the key elements of a differentiated approach in the curriculum?

- Why is such great emphasis now placed on setting learning targets?

School-based task

Select a piece of work which has been completed by a pupil who has a learning difficulty. Using this as a baseline, identify possible new targets for the child. Explain your strategy.

10 The Special Educational Needs Coordinator

By the end of this chapter you will:

- be familiar with the role and responsibilities of the SENCO;
- have insights into the skills and aptitudes required for the role;
- understand the benefits of working closely with your SENCO.

From 1994 every school was required to appoint a member of staff as Special Educational Needs Coordinator (SENCO). Specifically, the SENCO became responsible for:

- day-to-day management of SEN policy;
- liaising with and advising fellow teachers;
- coordinating provision for SEN;
- maintaining the SEN register and overseeing records;
- liaising with parents/carers of children with SEN;
- contributing to In-Service Education and Training (INSET);
- liaising with external agencies.

In the short time since 1994 the SENCO's role and work has assumed the utmost importance. In many primary schools, and in virtually all secondary schools, this position is a full-time post, requiring skills of collaboration, good management and delegation as well as an ability to interact well with a wide range of people (other teachers, LSAs/TAs, parents/carers and children, educational psychologists, LEA representatives and so on). As with other aspects of the original Code, the role of SENCO has gradually been refined.

A clear set of expectations have now been made explicit in the *National Standards for Special Educational Needs Coordinators* (TTA, 1998).

www http://www.canteach.gov.uk/info/library/sen.pdf

Among these it is stated that the SENCO is responsible for four key areas of SEN coordination:

47

A. Strategic direction and development of SEN in the school;
B. Teaching and Learning;
C. Leading and managing staff;
D. Efficient/effective deployment of staff/resources.

The Standards suggest that to be effective in coordinating each of these areas, a SENCO will need to demonstrate certain skills and attributes, namely

- leadership skills;
- decision-making skills;
- communication skills;
- self-management.

It is clear, then, that much is expected of the SENCO. The responsibilities of the role are reflected in the fact that many SENCOs are members of the senior management team in a large number of schools. The new Code summarises these responsibilities as follows:

- overseeing the day-to-day operation of the school's SEN policy;
- coordinating provision for children with SEN;
- liaising with and advising fellow teachers;
- managing LSAs;
- overseeing the records on all children with SEN;
- liaising with parents/carers of children with SEN;
- contributing to the in-service training of staff;
- liaising with external agencies.

SENCOs are clearly busy people, and have wide-ranging responsibilities. As a student teacher or NQT you should recognise this when seeking information or advice. Most SENCOs have a wealth of experience to offer you with regard to SEN, and by working closely with her you will gradually build up your own repertoire of skills and resources. SENCOs greatly appreciate the support and input of class teachers and are a great source of valuable knowledge and insight for the student or the NQT. And as we have indicated in Chapter 9, your responsibility as a class teacher is to assist the SENCO in monitoring and evaluating IEPs. So do not be afraid either to offer support or to ask for it! But remember – it will not always be possible for the SENCO to respond immediately to your request for assistance, so try to be patient.

Perhaps in recognition of the fact that the time required for SEN coordination is substantial, the new Code of Practice includes guidance to head teachers regarding the SENCO's timetable. As far as primary schools are concerned, for instance, it states that 'the SENCO role is at least equivalent to that of curriculum, literacy or numeracy coordinator'. Similarly, in secondary schools the role equates to that of the head of a large department. Information and Communications Technology (ICT) is seen as a major benefit to the SENCO, in terms of providing support for the management systems needed to organise effective SEN input, as well as for such things as IEPs, SEN registers and so on.

Some idea of the complexity of the role of SENCO may be gathered by referring to Appendix 9, which shows how wide ranging a SENCO's responsibilities are. You can obtain further information and insights on the SENCO's role, and on some of the day-to-day issues which arise, by accessing the SENCO Forum web-site.

`www` **http://forum.ngfl.gov.uk/senco-forum/**

Check out in particular its archive pages, to give you an idea of the wide range of issues that SENCOs routinely have to deal with.

Key reference

Farrell, M. (1998) 'The role of the special educational needs coordinator: Looking forward', *Support for Learning* **13** (2), 82–6.

Michael Farrell reviews the literature, research and legislation regarding SENCOs. He believes that massive expectations are placed on SENCOs, but believes that the work will gradually become more manageable – though not less important.

Supporting references

Davies, J., Garner, P. and Lee, J. (1999) 'Special educational needs co-ordinators and the Code: No longer practising', *Support for Learning* **14** (1), 37–40.

Lewis, A. *et al.* (1997) 'SENCOs and the Code: A national survey', *Support for Learning* **12** (1), 3–9.

Wedell, K. *et al.* (1997) 'SENCOs sharing questions and answers', *British Journal of Special Education*, **24** (4), 167–70.

Key questions

- Do you think it is fair to suggest that the status of the SENCO has increased dramatically in the last ten years? Give reasons for your conclusion.

- How can the SENCO be of greatest assistance to an NQT?

- Which part of the SENCO's work do you feel is most important to you as a classroom teacher?

School-based task

You are asked to talk to a SENCO about her role. Try to obtain a personal insight into the range of tasks required and the time constraints that she frequently has to work to.

11 Contributing to Individual Education Plans (IEPs)

By the end of this chapter you will:

- understand the function and importance of IEPs;
- recognise the key elements of an effective IEP;
- recognise some of the ways in which you can use an IEP effectively.

Individual Education Plans (IEPs) have become central to effectively planning to meet the needs of children with SEN. Although they have been around for a very long time in special schools, their widespread use for children with SEN in mainstream settings was heralded in the 1994 Code of Practice. This recommended that all children who are at Stages 2 and 3 should have an IEP. Under the most recent arrangements, children at both School Action and School Action Plus will have an IEP.

An IEP is a tool which helps teachers to plan and teach children with SEN. It focuses on a set of learning 'targets', and provides teachers with details of how these are likely to be met, and in what timescale. The classroom teacher has a key role in developing the IEP (see Chapter 9).

There have been a large number of refinements in the format and use of IEPs since 1994. Much useful advice is to be found, for example, in the DfEE's SEN Good Practice Guide (1999). www http://www.dfee.gov.uk/sen/sen_iep.htm

We now accept that effective IEPs should:

- be seen as a working document;
- use a simple format;
- specify *only* additional targets;
- avoid jargon;
- be comprehensible to staff and parents/carers;
- be distributed to all staff;
- promote effective planning;
- help pupils understand their own progress;
- result in action/specific learning goals.

The Code of Practice (DfEE, 2001) offers a succinct guide to what information an IEP should include:

- the short-term targets set for the child;
- the teaching strategies to be used;
- the provision to be put in place;
- when the plan is to be reviewed;
- the outcome of the action taken.

The Revised Code states that 'The IEP should only record that which is additional to or different from the differentiated curriculum plan, which is in place as part of provision for all children' (p. 34). It also advises us that the IEP should:

- be crisply written;
- focus on only 3–4 targets;
- be discussed with both the child and his parents/carers;
- be reviewed at least twice each year.

It is possible that you may encounter one variant to the IEP – the somewhat oddly titled 'Group IEP'. This is sometimes used in schools when a small group of pupils work together on a set of predetermined learning targets. Although the targets are the same, individual pupils might achieve them at different rates. This process certainly helps to curtail the amount of paperwork, while ensuring that a school's responsibilities are fulfilled. In developing Group IEPs you should follow the same guidance provided for IEPs.

One of the keys to the development of effective IEPs is the ability to set appropriate targets. Some of the ways in which you can develop skills in this area are discussed in Chapter 11.

If all of the features described above are taken on board you will be left with an IEP which will accrue real benefits, principally in helping to raise the achievement level of a pupil who has a learning difficulty. Remember, too, that IEPs contribute to your own development, in enabling you to target your teaching efforts more accurately. In summarising the wide range of positive outcomes of the effective use of IEPs we can say that IEPs will:

- enhance learning opportunities for SEN pupils;
- help to develop support for SEN pupils;
- identify those key skills which enable SEN pupils to access the whole curriculum;
- identify clear roles and responsibilities for all those teachers concerned with IEPs;
- ensure a collaborative educational effort to meet a pupil's SEN;
- establish common goals for the pupil through target setting;
- present important opportunities for staff development.

But what does an IEP actually look like? We have included some examples of IEPs in Appendix 7. To be effective an IEP will:

- be brief and action based;
- indicate the pupil's current levels of achievement;
- identify the nature, extent and specific areas of a pupil's learning difficulty;
- specify the learning programme and set specific relevant targets to be achieved;
- represent achievable goals;
- specify any other additional support or resources;
- indicate how parents/carers will be involved;
- include contributions from the pupil;
- outline any additional requirements such as medical or counselling needs;
- clarify monitoring and recording arrangements with dates;
- establish a timetable for review.

Key reference

Tod, J. (1999) 'IEPs: Inclusive Educational Practices?', *Support for Learning* **14** (4), 184–8.

This article reviews developments in IEPs. The author believes that reliability and validity of IEP content is crucial if it is to effectively support educational inclusion. IEPs, moreover, need to be firmly embedded in the work that teachers do in the classroom.

Supporting references

Cooper, P. (1996) 'Are Individual Education Plans a waste of paper?', *British Journal of Special Education* **23** (3), 115–19.

Goddard, A. (1997) 'The role of individual education plans/programmes in special education: A critique', *Support for Learning* **12** (4), 170–4.

Pearson, S. (2000) 'The relationship between school culture and individual education plans', *British Journal of Special Education* **27** (3), 145–9.

Key questions

- Does an emphasis on 'individual' planning seem to run contrary to the principle of educational inclusion – or does it support it? Give some reasons for your judgement.

- How best can an NQT contribute to IEPs?

- What is the importance of jointly planning the content and review of IEPs?

School-based task

Obtain a copy of an existing (blank) IEP. Assess its strengths and indicate how you might make best use of it as a class teacher.

12 The school SEN policy

By the end of this chapter you will:

- be aware of the importance of a school's SEN policy;
- recognise the required content of an SEN policy;
- understand what the SEN policy means for you.

All schools must have a written SEN policy whose content should broadly conform to the guidance laid out in the Code of Practice (DfEE, 2001). As part of their statutory duties, governing bodies of all maintained mainstream schools must publish information about the school's policy on SEN to parents/carers and others. The specific requirements on coverage are laid down in The Education (Special Educational Needs) (Information) Regulations 1994, and formal guidance was set out in Circular 6/94. Good practice suggests that while the governing body and the head teacher will take overall responsibility for the school's SEN policy, the school as a whole should be involved in its development. As with all other school policies, the SEN policy should be subject to a regular cycle of monitoring, evaluation and review. The school should consider whether the policy needs amending in the light of this process.

The SEN policy is essentially a statement of the school's philosophy, intent, strategic planning and current practices regarding SEN. It is intended for the information and use of governors, all staff and parents/carers. The policy can also form the basis of professional development activity for teachers and LSAs. It can also be used to outline particular strengths, successes or specialisms in SEN.

A whole-school approach

The SEN policy should reflect both the practice and aspirations of the whole school and involve all members of the school in its development. While this is often difficult to organise, the benefits in terms of 'ownership' of the policy are clear. So right from the outset there is an opportunity for NQTs to have a say in the policy.

As with other aspects of SEN provision, there has been a good deal of refinement in our thinking about what comprises a 'good' SEN policy. The original Code of Practice was helpful in establishing a set of key elements of an effective policy, as follows:

1. Basic information about the school's special educational provision

- objectives of the school's SEN policy;
- name of the school's SEN coordinator or teacher responsible for the day-to-day operation of the SEN policy;
- the arrangements for coordinating educational provision for pupils with SEN;
- admission arrangements;
- any SEN specialism and any special units;
- any special facilities which increase or assist access to the school by pupils with SEN.

2. Information about the school's policies for identification, assessment and provision for all pupils with SEN

- the allocation of resources to and among pupils with SEN;
- identification and assessment arrangements; and review procedures;
- arrangements for providing access for pupils with SEN to a balanced and broadly based curriculum, including the National Curriculum;
- how children with special educational needs are integrated within the school as a whole;
- criteria for evaluating the success of the school's SEN policy;
- arrangements for considering complaints about special educational provision within the school.

3. Information about the school's staffing policies and partnership with bodies beyond the school

- the school's arrangements for SEN in-service training;
- use made of teachers and facilities from outside the school, including support services;
- arrangements for partnership with parents/carers;
- links with other mainstream schools and special schools, including arrangements when pupils change schools or leave school;
- links with health and social services, educational welfare services and any voluntary organisations.

An example of one school's SEN policy is contained in Appendix 8. This example provides an illustration of the type and complexity of information that needs to be made available to everybody in the school. During the period following the introduction of the initial Code of Practice, most schools gradually refined their documentation and many, like the one we illustrate, have become helpful working documents.

There have been numerous critiques of school SEN policies since 1994, and these have led to some helpful suggestions as to the manner in which this information is communicated. One useful source is summarised in the key reading for this chapter. Its authors, Jane Tarr and Gary Thomas, drew on a national survey of school SEN policies. They found that there has been considerable progress made in the refinement of school SEN policies in line with the requirements of the Code of Practice (1994), the Education (Special Educational Needs) (Information) Regulations 1994 and in part 1 of Circular 6/94, which deals with the organisation of SEN provision in schools. These requirements have been identified in the preceding paragraphs in this chapter and were neatly summarised by Tarr and Thomas as relating to 14 main headings:

Principles and objectives (of the school)
SENCO's name and role
Strategic management and target setting (in SEN)
Admissions policy
Specialisms (e.g. a resource unit for children with hearing impairments)
Resource allocation
Identification, assessment and review procedures
Curriculum approaches
Integration strategies
Complaints: how parents/carers can query SEN issues in the school
INSET and staff development
External support
Parents/carers
Transition arrangements (e.g. from KS2 to KS3 and from KS4 to further education).

Most teachers will agree that the benefits of having a policy for SEN are only realised if the written document is a 'working' document which is the subject of ongoing scrutiny and review. As an NQT you will be expected to participate in this process. One of the significant benefits of this is the development of whole-school 'ownership' of the policy's contents, a matter to which we have already referred. This allows for common understandings and shared approaches to materialise: these, as any experienced teacher will tell you, are vital to the establishment and enhancement of a positive school ethos and effective provision for SEN pupils.

While there has undoubtedly been considerable progress made in refining school SEN policies a number of concerns remain. These are both practical and philosophical. The former relate especially to two things (i) audience and (ii) strategic direction and finance, while the latter raises the important issue of the SEN policy in respect of inclusion. We will now briefly consider each of these matters.

In developing a written school policy for SEN it is important to bear in mind who is the audience. Teachers, for example, are likely to need a more detailed version of a school policy than parents/carers, though the full policy should be available for any parent who requests a copy. So it is essential that teachers should have at the front of their minds the varied backgrounds of governors and helpers when developing or refining the policy. As we have already observed, SEN is rife with acronyms, jargon and technical language, the use of which sometimes inhibits understanding. They should therefore be avoided.

According to Tarr and Thomas (1997), one of the key weaknesses in many SEN policies was an absence of information regarding strategic management and finance. The strategic issue is of great importance at the present time, in the light of the rapid changes taking place in SEN provision – not least in respect of more widespread educational inclusion. Thus, the policy needs to be dynamic and forward thinking: indeed, there have been suggestions that each school should have a 'policy review team' to ensure that this approach is developed.

It is also the case that the SEN policy should be transparent about resources. It is now recognised that the school SEN policy should give clear information about the allocation of such resources so that governors and others can check on the use of resources. Moreover, there are strong arguments for suggesting that if the policy is explicit about funding, SENCOs will be in a far better position to negotiate more effectively for additional time to be allotted to them for their role, or for resources to be targeted at particular needs.

Our second SEN policy discussion-point concerns the very existence of the SEN policy. Some commentators, for instance, would regard the existence of a discrete SEN-related policy to be non-inclusive. Far better, it could be argued, that schools should develop policies which are directed towards meeting the 'individual' (rather than 'special') needs of its pupils. It is likely that, as progression towards more fully inclusive schools gathers pace, this matter will become the subject of increasing and widespread discussion.

Finally, you are asked to examine the specimen school SEN policy in Appendix 8. Indeed, you may wish to assess the ways in which it meets the guidance on 'content' by Tarr and Thomas and discussed in this chapter.

Key reference

Tarr, J. and Thomas, G. (1997) 'The quality of SEN policies: Time for review?', *Support for Learning* **12** (1), 10–14.

The authors report on a survey of SEN policies. They indicate the progress that has been made, while identifying some of the difficulties that schools have had in constructing policies which meet official requirements. The article contains some practical advice on how schools can more easily meet their statutory obligation regarding written SEN policies.

Supporting references

Palmer, C. *et al.* (1994) 'The Four Ps of Policy', *British Journal of Special Education* **21**, (1), 4–6.

Facherty, A. *et al.* (1992) 'What you need is a policy...', *Educational Psychology in Practice* **7** (4), 237–8.

Ainscow, M. *et al.* (1999) 'The role of LEAs in developing inclusive policies and practices', *British Journal of Special Education* **26** (3), 136–40.

Key questions
• Why is a written policy for SEN so important for an NQT?
• Why is it sometimes difficult for schools to put 'policy' into 'practice'?
• Is the existence of an SEN policy in schools commensurate with moves towards educational inclusion?

School-based task
• Obtain a copy of a school's SEN policy. Scrutinise it according to the 14 key elements identified by Tarr and Thomas. What appear to be the policy's strengths?

PART THREE

Core Issues for Student Teachers

13 SEN and the curriculum

> By the end of this chapter you will:
>
> - be aware of the importance of the concept of 'curriculum access for all';
> - be alert to the need to take account of a pupil's learning style;
> - be familiar with key features of differentiated approaches.

The 1988 Education Act emphasised the importance of access to the National Curriculum (NC) for *all* children. Initially it was emphasised that parts of the National Curriculum may be modified or that some children could be 'disapplied', especially in cases of severe and complex SENs. As it turned out, however, very few children have remained outside of the NC, and this has especially been the case recently, with the introduction of 'P Scales'. These are standardised achievement levels issued by the DfEE in 2001 and are one means of assessing the level of achievement of those children whose learning difficulties are such that they are working below NC Level 1. It has become usual to refer to such children as 'working *towards* Level 1', thereby presenting a more positive description of their position. You can obtain further details of the 'P Scales' from the QCA web site.

www http://www.qca.org.uk/

Among the original NC documents were several dealing with SEN. In particular, *Curriculum Guidance 2: A Curriculum for All* (NCC, 1989) does contain some very useful basic information regarding differentiation, while a second pamphlet, *Curriculum Guidance 9: The National Curriculum and Children with Severe Learning Difficulties* (NCC, 1992), promotes access to the NC for children with severe disabilities. We will be returning to the first of these booklets later in this chapter.

The last ten years has seen a rapid increase in the volume of literature concerning curriculum access, and especially differentiation. And it seems likely that this focus will prevail into the new millennium, as the focus on inclusion is sustained. Our focus, in this chapter, is principally on differentiation.

Differentiation

Differentiation of learning activities within the curriculum is an essential component of teaching. While it is a prerequisite strategy for all learners it has particular implications for those with SEN. One starting point for a consideration of differentiation is to consider it as a response to the different learning styles of children in your classroom. There has been a great deal of attention paid in recent years to this issue. This is important because there is a tendency (among all of us) to teach according to our own *preferred* style of learning. Let us consider a simple example. If you are asked for some information about a pupil you might:

- forget his name, but remember what he looks like (visual learning style);
- remember his name, but be unable to recognise him (auditory learning style);
- recall a situation, place or activity which involved the pupil (kinaesthetic/tactile learning style).

The key features of these learning styles are as follows:

The visual learner

- enjoys drawing, writing;
- observes in detail;
- has a good visual memory;
- uses graphics (charts, diagrams) to assist learning.

The auditory learner

- listens attentively;
- remembers verbal instructions/information;
- explains to others;
- enjoys drama, role-play and other oral activity.

The kinaesthetic learner

- likes practical/tactile activity;
- learns by 'doing';
- tends to resist non-practical activity;
- enjoys tactile and other sensory stimulation.

As with other summaries contained in this book, be aware that what we describe above is only a general indication of some of the things that you can look for. And you should recognise that most children will have some elements of each learning style, even though one will be predominant.

Now apply this simple categorisation of learning styles to a group of children. When presented with a particular task, they will all 'learn' differently, according to their preferred style. One important issue here, which has been identified as having a bearing on the high proportion of boys who experience SENs, is that many boys are more 'spatial' in the way that they approach a learning task. A teacher who places major emphasis on literacy skills alone in the curriculum, with an attendant requirement that any 'reporting' of work done should be in written form, places such boys at a considerable disadvantage. As a classroom teacher, therefore, you need to be conscious of providing optional activities and experiences to enable children to access the National Curriculum.

The advice about differentiation is, of course, applicable to all Key Stages. Before looking at some of the more general issues concerning curriculum approaches it is timely to reinforce what the Revised Code of Practice has to say about the secondary school curriculum. In particular, it emphasises the need for individual subject teachers to assess the level of achievement and progress made by a child within their own subject area. As it comments: 'It should be noted that an individual pupil may progress at different rates in different subject areas and thus consideration of placement in a set should be made subject by subject' (p. 42). It is crucial to bear this in mind when planning your teaching approach.

Curriculum Guidance 2: A Curriculum for All (NCC, 1989) provided some important guidelines regarding differentiated approaches. Like the work of the Warnock Commission ten years or so before it, this document, we consider, is significant in heralding a challenge to all teachers to adapt their curricular approaches to enable more widespread access. Thus, *Curriculum Guidance 2* rested on the principle that 'All pupils share the right to a broad and balanced curriculum, including the National Curriculum' (p. 1), while providing a salutory reminder that 'The right to share in the curriculum...does not automatically ensure access to it, or progress within it' (p. 1).

The document goes on to provide some useful, general advice which, we maintain, has substantial currency at the present time. Two sections are of particular interest to the student teacher, and we provide an amended summary of these below.

The learning environment

Does the way in which you orchestrate learning promote:

- an atmosphere of encouragement, acceptance and respect for the individual needs of all?
- positive pupil–teacher interactions and adjustments to changing needs?
- easy access to resources, including ICT?
- flexible grouping of pupils?
- management of pupil behaviour via a whole-class approach?
- cooperative learning among pupils?
- effective collaboration with others (especially LSAs/TAs)?
- continuous liaison with parents/carers?

Pupils' teaching needs

Is your approach to curriculum 'delivery' based on:

- positive attitudes towards all children?
- partnerships with the learner?
- a climate of warmth and support which fosters confidence?
- encouraging all children to risk making mistakes as they learn?
- emphasising self-assessment?

The characteristics outlined above should be your core values in enabling access for all. They are premised by the somewhat old-fashioned notion of 'prizing the learner' – by providing the conditions whereby he can succeed. Obviously there is much more to 'differentiation' than that – far too much to elaborate here. Differentiation, traditionally, is located around an understanding that teachers have to accommodate the 'different' ways, rates and levels that children go about their academic and social learning in school. So you are encouraged to reflect on your own approach: are you ensuring that individual differences are being catered for by your:

- curriculum planning (e.g. range/level of content; range of activities/tasks; pupil-interest; IEP targets)?
- your teaching (structure; clarity; pace; teaching style; pupil grouping; support)?
- how you assess levels of achievement (pupil feedback; reviewing IEP targets; 'teacher judgement').

You will notice that we have purposely avoided reference to any 'technical' aspects of the National Curriculum in this chapter. The content of NC documentation is, as we have indicated earlier, applicable to all learners, and should be read by you with this in mind. Nor have we dealt with such increasingly important issues as target-setting for pupils working towards Level 1 of the National Curriculum, the 'P Scales' – as briefly mentioned earlier in this chapter.

Finally, it is crucial to bear in mind that the most recent National Curriculum documents, with which you will become increasingly familiar, are explicit in their statements concerning the inclusion of all *learners*.

www **http://www.dfee.gov.uk/a-z/CURRICULUM.html**.

These begin by stating that the aim of the school curriculum is to:

- provide opportunities for all pupils to learn and achieve;
- promote pupils' spiritual, moral, social and cultural development and prepare all pupils for the opportunities, responsibilities and experiences of life.

But even more relevant to the pupil who has a learning difficulty is the advice given in the NC documentation, which indicates that teachers should 'provide all pupils with relevant and appropriately challenging work at each key stage'. It also requires teachers to have due regard to three core principles in developing more inclusive curricular approaches:

- setting suitable learning challenges;
- responding to pupils' diverse learning needs;
- overcoming potential barriers to learning and assessment for individuals and groups of pupils.

Further details of these approaches, and examples of how they operate in practice, are available from the National Curriculum handbooks.

The content of this chapter can be usefully cross-referenced with our comments in Chapters 7, 9, 11 and 15, and by examining Appendices 6 and 10.

Key reference

O'Brien, T. (1998) 'The millenium curriculum: Confronting the issues and proposing solutions', *Support for Learning* **13 (4)**, 147–52.

Tim O'Brien offers some clues to the future directions of curriculum thinking in SEN. He suggests that teachers need to return to being more expansive about what they regard as 'the curriculum', and discusses the curricular implications inherent in meeting individual needs, differentiation and inclusion.

Supporting references

Blamires, M. (1999) 'Universal design for learning: re-establishing differentiation as part of the inclusion agenda?', *Support for Learning* **14 (4)**, 158–63.

Ollerton, M. (2001) 'Inclusion and entitlement, equality of opportunity and quality of curriculum provision', *Support for Learning* **16 (1)**, 35–40.

Weston, P. (1992) 'A Decade of Differentiation', *British Journal of Special Education* **19 (1)**, 6–9.

Key questions

- What are some of the ways in which 'access for all' can be ensured?

- Describe what is meant by 'differentiation'

- What are the benefits of enabling a severely disabled child to have access to the full curriculum?

School-based task

Describe some of the ways in which your placement school tries to enable curriculum access to all.

14 Pupil behaviour and SEN

By the end of this chapter you will:

- recognise the interdependence between behaviour, achievement and SEN;
- understand why some pupils behave inappropriately;
- be more aware of some of the strategies you can adopt to minimise unwanted behaviour;
- be clear about the importance of (i) the whole-school behaviour policy and (ii) the need to provide opportunities for pupils to participate in managing their own behaviour.

The relationship between pupil behaviour (and by this term we always seem to mean *inappropriate* behaviour – an interpretation which is a talking point in itself) and SEN is a close one. This does not just apply to those children who are regarded as having 'emotional and behavioural difficulties' (EBD). When we examine the range of learners in any classroom we will encounter differences in learning styles, personalities, levels of achievement, social skills and backgrounds. All of these things, to some extent, will have an impact on the way in which children behave. Nevertheless, there appear to be some close correlations between the existence of unwanted 'problem' behaviours and underachievement. So it is important at the outset to establish a number of baseline guiding principles, such as:

- Do not assume that the pupil alone has 'the problem'.
- Early recognition, followed by intervention is essential – action, rather than reaction.
- Do not make assumptions about a child on the basis of hearsay or anecdote.
- Collect evidence of 'problems' to support positive actions.
- Problem behaviour is not normally towards an individual, but directed at 'systems'.
- Ensure that you 'listen' to children – even when you're under pressure.

There has been a history of recent concern in respect of children regarded as having EBD. In 1989 a far-reaching government enquiry on 'discipline in schools' (the Elton Report) concluded that there was no widespread indiscipline in schools – indeed, the most problematic behaviour reported by teachers in the research that supported the Report was 'talking out of turn' (DES, 1989). In 1994 a series of circulars were published, providing guidance to teachers on discipline, EBD, exclusions and other related issues.

As the 1990s have progressed, concern has been heightened because of two themes: the measurement of school performance in 'league tables' and the gathering pace of educational inclusion. It is accurate to suggest that a debate has been ongoing regarding the compatibility of these two issues. Certainly, there are many teachers who subscribe to a view that (i) the educational inclusion of children who present severely challenging (EBD) behaviours is virtually impossible and (ii) such children are inclined to inhibit the overall educational performance of the school in any case.

It is probably fair to say that, of all learners, those children whose SENs are deemed to be EBD-related, present teachers and schools with the greatest challenge – and not a little controversy along the way. It was therefore hardly a surprise that the Programme of Action highlighted this group for focused attention. Moreover, there have been a series of concerted initiatives to increase the levels of social inclusion of previously marginalised groups (of which EBD pupils are one). You can access one example by going to this web-site:

www **http://www.dfee.gov.uk/sen/nagsen.htm**

This provides you with details of the development of a national strategy for the education of pupils who are viewed as falling into the EBD grouping.

It is important to recognise that concerns about children who frequently behave in ways which are inappropriate have been a salient characteristic of schooling for a very long time: there are historical precedents for the existence of disaffected, alienated young people within the school system. In other words, problem behaviour by pupils is not a new phenomenon!

Words of caution – definitions...categories again!

Children who are regarded as having an 'emotional or behavioural difficulty' are representative of one point of a continuum of behaviours which range from what the DfE called 'unacceptable though normal' through to 'serious mental illness' (DFE, 1994). EBD falls somewhere in the middle of this continuum. But in making this observation we need to add some words of caution.

The pupil 'group' to which we refer have over the years been subject to perhaps the worst of all the excesses of 'categorisation'. The language used in relation to pupil behaviour is frequently loaded with (mainly unwanted) meaning: thus, we talk about 'discipline', 'classroom control', 'punishment' and so on. And looking back through our own involvement in this aspect of special education, we have witnessed the widespread use of such terms as 'maladjusted', 'disruptive', 'disturbed', and 'deviant'. What is noteworthy is that such terms have been afforded a kind of quasi-scientific status – certainly a status not in keeping with their subjectivity. And even when a recently popularised umbrella term for such pupils is used with official sanction ('pupils with problems'), there seems little doubt that there is a built-in assumption that it is solely the child who has the 'problem'. In our experience this is not always the case.

Remember, too, that all 'behaviour' has to be viewed as 'behaviour in context'. This means that what might be acceptable in one location is not necessarily so in another. Similarly, no two persons' description or interpretation of a behaviour will ever be the same. While schools work hard to minimise the difficulties posed by 'behaviour in context', both are nevertheless further complicating issues for all teachers, new or experienced.

Moreover, there is an unfortunate tendency to assume that a child who is termed 'disruptive' or 'a problem' on account of his behaviour is always behaving in an unacceptable or inappropriate manner. Again, this is seldom the case. So, as a starting point for this section we would urge you to identify the strengths or positive features that the child has. As with other aspects of learning, these can become the focal point of intervention.

Looking for causes

When a child fails to behave in a manner which allows his learning and that of others to progress it is important to try to 'problem solve' the circumstances for this. It is likely that there are a combination of factors – and again you must avoid jumping to conclusions based on what is immediately apparent. Broadly speaking there are three groups of potential, often interlinked, causes. In the diagram below we keep these brief, leaving you to provide further potential causes under each sub-heading.

---

1. **Organic**
   - Illness
   - Sensory/physical impairment
   - Cognitive delay

2. **Psychological**
   - Lack of confidence
   - Poor self-esteem
   - Poor social skills

3. **Environmental/social**
   - Family factors
   - School-related factors
   - Influence of sub-cultures

Understanding the reason why a pupil misbehaves is an important part of being able to deal effectively with the problems such actions create – and don't forget that there will be at least four groups affected by unacceptable behaviour:

- the child;
- his parents/carers;
- the teacher;
- other children.

An excellent source for guidance, for students and qualified teachers alike, relating to the management of children who are more inclined to behave in ways which are unacceptable, can be found in DFE Circular 9/94.

www **http://www.dfee.gov.uk/sen/circ994.htm**

At this point we want to consider two key issues, both of which will have an important bearing on your work.

Whole-school issues

An accompanying piece of guidance to that of Circular 9/94 was that relating to pupil behaviour and discipline – Circular 8/94, which has now been largely superseded. This stated that all schools should have a written behaviour policy to reflect schools' vision and values relating to: respect for others; respect for property and the environment; honesty; trust; fairness; tolerance; compassion; self-respect; and self-discipline.

The head teacher, acting on behalf of the governors, has the ultimate responsibility for a range of duties relating to the management of behaviour. These include:

- developing the school rules and code of conduct;
- promoting self-discipline and proper regard for authority;
- encouraging good behaviour and respect for others;
- ensuring standards for pupil behaviour are acceptable;
- regulating the conduct of pupils;
- making known within the school any matters that the governing body may decide upon regarding behaviour/discipline;
- consulting with the LEA before determining any measures arising from proposed measures which can be expected to:
  - a) lead to increased expenditure by the LEA;
  - b) affect the responsibility of the authority as an employer;
- the power to exclude a pupil.

Good practice, and evidence from schools which has demonstrated an ability to engender pro-social attitudes among even the most disaffected children, indicates that the whole-school behaviour policy can promote good behaviour by a set of simple rules that are clearly understood by pupils, parents/carers and school staff.

Moreover, behaviour policies should be:

- regularly reviewed;
- worked out collaboratively, involving the whole school – teaching and non-teaching staff;

- discussed with parents/carers and pupils;
- feature in the annual report to parents/carers.

Furthermore, the key elements underpinning the policy should feature in the school prospectus. At its most basic, few teachers would disagree that perhaps the core consideration here is encouraging respect for others. There should be an agreed understanding, among staff, pupils and parents/carers, of what is important, to be valued, tolerated and deemed acceptable behaviour.

The individual teacher

Received wisdom, and suggestions contained in Circular 8/94, indicate that schools and individual teachers can help to sustain positive relationships by considering the following:

- positive recognition for acts of consideration;
- engaging older pupils in caring for younger and disadvantaged pupils;
- curricular focus on such issues;
- drawing commendable behaviour to the attention of parents/carers;
- prizes for the same;
- offering an effective, differentiated curriculum;
- high expectations by teachers;
- constructive, positive discipline code;
- clear understanding by pupils of expected discussion and participation in lessons; movement in class; practice for handing work in; action to be taken when work is completed;
- clear explanations;
- ensuring that the work requirements of pupils are clearly set out;
- misbehaviour handled quickly and calmly;
- teachers using good listening skills;
- appropriate work set;
- clear goals for each activity;
- lessons start and end on time;
- classroom suited for activity where possible;
- suitable seating arrangements;
- minimal external interruptions where possible;
- materials for activities available.

You should also be aiming to secure a balance between rewards and punishments (more frequently referred to as 'sanctions'). Such rewards typically include:

Public commendation
Merit marks or certificates
Letters home
Appropriate entries in homework and exercise books

Prominent display of pupils' work
Personal log or day book
'Quiet' praise.

A further source of up-to-date information and advice is the DfEE Circular dealing with combating disaffection. **www** **http://www.dfee.gov.uk/circulars/10-99/combat.htm** This site contains some excellent examples of how to tackle those situations in which pupil disaffection has become more pronounced. In particular it provides advice on the setting up of Pastoral Support Programmes (PSP) for such young people, together with advice concerning inter-agency collaboration. This information can usefully be read alongside the content of the Circular on social inclusion.

www **http://www.dfee.gov.uk/circulars/11-99/11-99.htm**

And finally, a note of reassurance! As the Elton Report (DES, 1989) points out, you will never be able to *completely* eradicate problematic behaviours. All you can reasonably be expected to do is to manage problems with commonsense, tact and sensitivity – while bearing in mind the need for consistency and firmness. Above all, where SEN is concerned, behaviours which are challenging or difficult for the teacher are often the surface manifestation of more deep-seated learning difficulties. As with other SENs, therefore, continue to seek advice on this most controversial and (at times) stressful phenomenon.

Key reference

Gray, P. and Panter, S. (2000) 'Exclusion or inclusion? A perspective on policy in England for pupils with emotional and behavioural difficulties', *Support for Learning* **15** (1), 4–7.

The authors offer a review of recent government initiatives on pupil behaviour. While recognising that much positive work has been done to include pupils with EBD, Gray and Panter believe that other legislation militates against further success.

Supporting references

Richards, I. (1999) 'Inclusive schools for pupils with emotional and behavioural difficulties', *Support for Learning* **14** (3), 99–104.
Cole, T. and Visser, J. (1998) 'How Should the "Effectiveness" of Schools for Pupils with EBD be Assessed?', *Emotional and Behavioural Difficulties* **3** (1), 37–43.
Cooper, P. (1996) 'Giving it a Name: the value of descriptive categories in educational approaches to emotional and behavioural difficulties', *Support for Learning* **11** (4) 146–50.

Key questions

- How can EBD pupils be effectively included within mainstream educational settings?

- How far is it fair to say that environmental/social factors play a greater causal part in problem behaviour than do individual factors?

- Should poorly behaved children be 'rewarded' if they begin to behave in a more appropriate way? Give some reasons for your response.

School-based task

Obtain a copy of a school's behaviour policy. What aspects of it are especially
helpful to you as a student teacher who will soon be working full time in school?

15 Developing your inclusive thinking

By the end of this chapter you will:

- be more familiar with the recent developments in inclusive practice in education;
- formulate a viable definition of what constitutes 'inclusion' in education;
- review some of the approaches which enable educational inclusion;
- consider some of the benefits and challenges of including a wider range of learners in your classroom.

Inclusion has become a major theme in policy and practice in education systems world-wide over the last decade. Its roots go back much further in history, with the work of progressive educationists and movements who have sought to respond to the increasingly exclusionary and competitive stance taken by society towards disabled people and those whose pattern of learning and behaviour makes them in some way different from those around them. More recent history, as we have noted, has been characterised by the impact on SEN of the Warnock Report and the subsequent 1981 Education Act, which heralded the first wide-ranging steps towards 'integration', itself a precursor to educational inclusion.

While recognising the importance of these distant and more recent historical precedents, the focus in this section is on the more recent past, attention to which allows us to trace some of the core principles underlying what is undoubtedly a key development for SEN.

At the outset we must clarify exactly what is meant by 'inclusion', a term which is variously used together with such adjectives as 'social' and 'educational', and often as a counterpoint to 'exclusion'. For the purposes of this book we focus mainly on 'educational inclusion' – though in Chapter 18 we suggest that issues relating to 'social inclusion' need to be an integral part of any teacher's thinking.

Let us begin then by examining the term 'inclusion'. In a helpful mapping of the distinction between 'traditional' and more inclusive approaches in education, one observer (Porter, 1995) identifies the following differences:

Traditional approaches	*Inclusion approaches*
Focus on pupil	Focus on classroom
Assessment of pupil by specialist	Examine teaching/learning factors
Diagnostic/prescriptive outcomes	Collaborative problem-solving
Pupil programme (of work)	Strategies for teachers
Placement in appropriate programme	Adaptive/supportive mainstream classes

One of the distinctions which needs to be made at an early stage is that between 'integration', which you will have read about earlier in connection with the Warnock Report and the 1981 Act, and inclusion. The former term placed the emphasis on the capacity of the child with SEN to assimilate the prevailing cultures, routines and expectations of the mainstream school. There was, within this approach, little which prompted the school to critique and change its own provision and procedures, in order to enable the SEN child to have access to all of its educational opportunities. What was provided were additional inputs or facilities for the SEN pupil: the school system remained unchanged. Educational inclusion, on the other hand, encourages schools to reconsider their overall structure, teaching approaches, pupil groupings and the use they make of support systems. In other words, fundamental change takes place which impacts on all members of the school community into which the pupil who experiences SEN becomes embedded.

So how do I make a start on the process of developing a more inclusive approach in the classroom? We are not going to attempt to repeat the very valuable advice provided by others here. The *Index for Inclusion* (CSIE, 2000) is, without doubt, the key document in this context, and we simply provide a summary of its key headings. Prior to that, however, it is worth reiterating the suggestions of Florian (1998) that among the most important considerations for the successful development of educational inclusion are:

- involving pupils in decision making;
- engendering a positive attitude to all learners;
- developing teacher knowledge about SENs and how to overcome them.

The *Index for Inclusion* covers three aspects or dimensions of schooling; each has a set of 'indicators', which can assist both in evaluating progress so far as well as helping to plan for future development. They are as follows.

Creating inclusive cultures

Building community

- everyone is made to feel welcome;
- students help each other;
- staff collaborate with each other;
- staff and students treat one another with respect;

- there is a partnership between staff and parents/carers;
- staff and governors work well together;
- all local communities are involved in the school.

Establishing inclusive values
- there are high expectations for all students;
- everyone shares a philosophy for inclusion;
- all students are equally valued;
- staff and students are treated as human beings as well as occupants of a 'role';
- staff seek to remove all barriers to learning and participation in school;
- the school strives to minimise discriminatory practices.

Producing inclusive policies

Developing a school for all
- staff appointments and promotions are fair;
- all new staff are helped to settle into the school;
- the school seeks to admit all students from its locality;
- the school makes its buildings physically accessible to all people;
- all students new to the school are helped to feel settled;
- the school arranges teaching groups so that all students are valued.

Organising support for diversity
- all forms of support are coordinated;
- staff development activities help staff to respond to student diversity;
- 'special needs' policies are inclusion policies;
- the Code of Practice is used to reduce the barriers to learning and participation of all students;
- support for those learning English as an additional language is coordinated with learning support;
- pastoral and behaviour support policies are linked to curriculum development and learning support policies;
- pressures for disciplinary exclusion are decreased;
- barriers to attendance are reduced;
- bullying is minimised.

Evolving inclusive practices

Orchestrating learning
- lessons are responsive to student diversity;
- lessons are made accessible to all students;
- lessons develop an understanding of difference;
- students are actively involved in their own learning;
- students learn collaboratively;
- assessment encourages the achievements of all students;

- classroom discipline is based on mutual respect;
- teachers plan, review and teach in partnership;
- teachers minimise barriers to learning and participation of all students;
- learning support assistants are concerned to support the learning and participation of all students;
- homework contributes to the learning of all;
- all students take part in activities outside the classroom.

Mobilising resources
- school resources are distributed fairly to support inclusion;
- community resources are known and drawn upon;
- staff expertise is fully utilised;
- student difference is used as a resource for teaching and learning;
- staff develop shared resources to support learning and participation.

It is clear, even from this summary, that the notion of inclusion extends far beyond SEN. It relates to all children and adults within the school community. Indeed, one of the hallmark differences between it and 'integration' is that the latter was a term which was specifically used in connection with SEN: inclusion is not.

As we have indicated elsewhere, inclusion is a challenging concept, but it is one which needs to be addressed in your own mind as you begin to engage with the practicalities of teaching. It is probably fair to say to those who see inclusion as 'problematic' that for every question raised about it there is most certainly a solution. What is equally certain is that the extent to which you feel able to persevere in the quest for these solutions (whether personal or institutional) will very much depend on being able to see beyond problems: educational inclusion brings with it widespread benefits, not least in helping teachers to refine and enhance their own practice.

Pupil participation

One important feature of inclusive practice in schools, and one which student teachers and NQTs can immediately make a contribution to, is the involvement of pupils in making decisions about their own education. All children and young people have rights, and yet the history of special education shows that disabled pupils and those with learning difficulties have frequently been marginalised. Currently, however, there is considerable emphasis placed on securing the rights of learners, including those who have SEN. Thus, the Code of Practice (2001) is unequivocal in this respect, using the UN Convention on the Rights of the Child as its guideline.

The United Nations Convention on the Rights of the Child, adopted by the General Assembly in 1989, and ratified by the United Kingdom in 1991, recognises in Articles 12, 13 and 23 that children have a right to obtain and make known information, to express an opinion, and to have that opinion taken into account in any matter or procedure affecting the child.

The Children Act 1989, however, states that the teacher has to arrive at

> a fine balance between giving the child a voice and encouraging them to make informed decisions, and overburdening them with decision-making procedures where they have insufficient experience and knowledge to make appropriate judgements without additional support.

One way of ensuring that this does not happen is to liaise effectively with parents/carers, using the guidance contained elsewhere in this book. This process needs very careful handling, as some parents/carers

> may be reluctant to involve their child in education decision-making perhaps considering them ill-equipped to grasp all the relevant factors...(and)...they may suspect that professionals may give undue weight to the views of their children.
>
> (Code of Practice, 2001, p. 14).

As a classroom teacher you can assist in the process of enabling the child to participate in his own learning by:

- providing clear, accurate and easily understood information about the child's SEN;
- indicating the purpose of any assessment, IEP and subsequent intervention;
- ensuring that the pupil understands the agreed outcomes of these procedures;
- explaining what additional support is being made and why;
- consulting with pupils to ensure that support provided is both timely and sensitive;
- ensuring that the pupil understands the role and contribution of any other professionals;
- being aware of any local pupil support or advocacy services for children;
- ensuring that the pupil can discuss any concerns with a nominated teacher or LSA;
- being aware of and sensitive to stress factors on the child as a result of his SEN.

Further advice regarding pupil participation in schools and other settings is available from the Code of Practice (2001):

www **http://www.dfee.gov.uk/sen/standard.htm**

and from the DfEE SEN good practice guidance:

www **http://www.dfee.gov.uk/circulars/dfeepub/jul00/020700/**

Lest you find some of the expectations contained in the *Index for Inclusion* (CSIE, 2000) a little daunting at first sight, you should recognise that it is generally considered that inclusion is a process, not a fixed state. The best that most of us can hope for in our teaching is that we can talk of 'working towards' greater inclusion. The process, in other words, is never-ending. We have included in our appendices two examples of ways in which your own developing insights and skills about inclusion might be assessed. But please do bear in mind that these are starting points only.

Key reference

Ainscow, M. (1997) 'Towards inclusive schooling', *British Journal of Special Education* **24** (1), 3–6.

Mel Ainscow offers an overview of the movement towards inclusion within education systems. He suggests a series of propositions about conditions to enable this, placing emphasis on teacher education in particular.

Supporting references

Knight, B. (1999) 'Towards inclusion of students with special educational needs in the regular classroom', *Support for Learning* **14** (1), 3–7.

Rose, R. *et al.* (1996) 'Promoting the greater involvement of pupils with special needs in the management of their own assessment and learning processes', *British Journal of Special Education* **23** (4), 166–71.

Hornby, G. (1999) 'Inclusion or delusion: Can one size fit all?', *Support for Learning* **14** (4), 152–7.

Key questions

- To what extent is educational inclusion beneficial for everyone?

- What difficulties might you foresee in promoting 'full' inclusion?

- How can 'inclusive schools' exist in a society which continues to marginalise some groups?

School-based task

Identify some of the characteristics of a school you have recently visited which, in your view, make it 'inclusive'.

16 Working with others

By the end of this chapter you will:

- be familiar with the range of other professionals that you are likely to work alongside in meeting SENs in school;
- be particularly aware of the work of the Learning Support Assistant/Teaching Assistant;
- identify aspects of 'good practice' in working with others.

One of the most important features of recent SEN provision is the need for teachers to work in collaboration with a range of other professionals – other teachers, Learning Support Assistants (LSAs)/Teaching Assistants (TAs), educational psychologists, social workers, speech therapists, child protection officers and so on. It will not be unusual, for example, for you to participate in a review meeting regarding a child with learning difficulty which includes several of these key individuals. You should not be overawed by this: your views are crucially important, as you will probably be the person who knows the child best. Other professionals will certainly take account of what you are saying.

In this chapter we focus mainly on your relationship with LSAs/TAs, as it is highly likely that both as a student and an NQT you will work in close contact with them. Before considering them, however, we will note briefly the main characteristics of the work of some non-teaching SEN support workers.

- The SEN Adviser/Inspector: employed by an LEA; usually provides support to a number of schools, and coordinates training and professional development on SEN issues. It is likely that you will encounter her in the first instance during your induction programme. The Inspector contributes to policy planning and review in SEN across the LEA.

- Peripatetic Support Teacher: usually works with children who are at School Action Plus. Broadly speaking they will fall into two groups: those with expertise in, and responsibility for, basic skills (literacy and numeracy) and those who specialise in supporting children whose special need is related to EBD. Both will be great sources of information for you, both about their specialist area and about SEN issues in general.

• Education Welfare Officer (EWO): is mainly involved in supporting children whose attendance causes concern or those who have a record of truancy. They liaise closely with the 'pastoral' staff, SENCO, parents/carers and other LEA services (the Educational Psychology Service in particular). They are immensely knowledgeable about social and emotional factors which often contribute to a pupil's learning difficulty.

• Speech and Language Specialist: works with children whose principal difficulties concern their use and understanding of language. Typically these might include children whose SEN relates to an 'autistic spectrum disorder'(ASD), or those whose difficulties are organically based (as in cases of some speech impairments) or cognitively based (in the case of global language delay). Speech and Language Specialists will tend to work mainly at School Action Plus Stage, and will once again be excellent sources of practical advice for teachers.

There are, of course, several other groups of professionals whose work is important in enabling children's needs to be met. Their absence from the examples we have provided above does not minimise their importance: indeed, we invite you to find out more about their roles in one of the activities at the end of this chapter.

It seems likely that the range of those working with children with learning difficulties will continue to expand. For example, Connexions, the government's support service for young people, is due to begin in 2001. Its goal is to ensure success through learning and a smooth transition to adulthood and working life for every young person. The programme will have particular relevance for young people who have learning difficulties. A key person in Connexions will be the mentor, who will provide support and guidance to youngsters at Key Stages 3 and 4.

wwwhttp://www.connexions.gov.uk/

Working with LSAs/TAs

Now let us turn to look in more detail at your work with LSAs/TAs. At the outset it is important to note that LSAs are increasingly referred to as 'teaching assistants', both in official literature and in some schools. For the sake of simplicity though, we will continue to use the term LSA/TA in this book. But whatever their title, there can be no doubt that this group has become immensely important. Indeed, the contribution of LSAs/TAs in helping to meet the SENs of pupils has been recognised – not least in the 1997 Green Paper, which led to the Programme of Action. Both highlight important features of the work of LSAs/TAs, as well as pointing to the need to enhance their training opportunities.

www http://www.dfee.gov.uk/sengp/index.htm

The LSA/TA can be of significant assistance to students and NQTs. One recent analysis of their role, for instance, suggests that 'Beginning teachers need to develop the pattern of support which works for them and cultivate the opportunities to talk over difficulties with experienced staff who have time to lend a listening ear. This person may very well be an LSA' (Bradley and Roaf, 2000, p. 191). Further information about the work of LSAs/TAs can be obtained by going to web-pages dealing with recent research on their role.

www **http://www.dfee.gov.uk/research/re_paper/RR161.doc**

We have also included an example of an LSA's/TA's job description in Appendix 11(i). An examination of this will give you some idea of how wide ranging an LSA's/ TA's duties now are. We have also included, in Appendix 11(ii) a proforma which is intended to help a classroom teacher to organise how she is going to use any extra adult help she might get in her classroom – it can be satisfactorily adapted for use with LSAs. But bear in mind that effective use of support requires the involvement of the adult helper in agreeing how support might best be given.

A number of children on the special needs register may well receive in-class support from an LSA/TA. Additionally, it should be noted, some schools will use volunteer helpers (often parents/carers) to support pupils who have SENs. So it is vital that such support is built into your planning of lessons and the way in which you are going to teach a class. There are some guiding principles for doing this. In all probability the school will have established some clear guidelines in this respect, and you should familiarise yourself with these. It may also be helpful if you examine a job description of an LSA/TA, in order to see the range of duties expected (see Appendix 11).

Typically, an LSA/TA will be involved in many of the following activities:

- helping the teacher to plan children's work;
- making suggestions regarding curriculum content;
- assisting in the preparation of curriculum materials;
- helping to organise the classroom to enable differentiated work;
- working with individuals or groups of children;
- contributing to, and supporting, a child's IEP;
- assisting with particular pupil tasks on a one-to-one basis;
- providing additional explanations to children;
- helping to keep children on task;
- supporting the teacher in general behaviour management;
- reviewing individual pupil progress in collaboration with the teacher;
- attending school briefings and professional development sessions;
- liaising with parents/carers, where appropriate.

These are just a few of a range of LSA/TA activities. What underscores every one of them is collaboration. The LSA's/TA's contribution to your own teaching will be immeasurably enhanced if you maintain a good level of daily communication with the LSA/TA. Thus, any LSA/TA that you work with will need to discuss with you some key elements such as:

- the way in which you interpret her role;
- your lesson plans and her role within them;
- your objectives for each part of a lesson;
- the LSA's/TA's role in behaviour management, classroom routines and organisation;
- the LSA's/TA's contribution to IEPs;
- guidelines regarding confidentiality;
- the purpose of any specific strategies you adopt with a pupil.

In order to achieve these things you will need to plan for regular meetings with the LSA/TA. Try to identify a specific time each week when you can discuss things. It is far better – and probably far more respectful to the LSA/TA – that such meetings are kept reasonably formal, rather than being hurried chats in the staffroom.

Key reference

Creese, A. *et al.* (1998) 'The prevalence and usefulness of collaborative teacher groups for SEN: Results of a national survey', *Support for Learning* **13** (3), 109–14.

The possibilities of collaboration between teachers in schools are explored in this article. The authors' findings are based on a large national survey, and indicate that this way of working is likely to be an important part in enhancing provision for SEN.

Supporting references

Margerison, A. (1997) 'Class teachers and the role of classroom assistants in the delivery of special educational needs', *Support for Learning* **12** (4), 166–9.
Wright, J. and Graham, J. (1997) 'Where and when do speech and language therapists work with teachers?', *British Journal of Special Education* **24** (4), 171–4.
Fletcher-Campbell, F. (1992) 'How can we use an extra pair of hands?', *British Journal of Special Education* **19** (4), 141–3.

Key questions

- Try to find out more about the work of the following:

  Educational psychologist

  Occupational therapist

  Parent Partnership Officer

- Identify some of the key features in establishing a good working relationship with them.

- What are the differences between the work of an LSA/TA and that of a teacher?

School-based task

Obtain a copy of an LSA's/TA's job description. What are its most significant features?

17 Relating to parents/carers

By the end of this chapter you will:

- understand the statutory requirements for involving parents/carers;
- be aware of the importance of good working relationships with parents/carers;
- develop more effective ways of communicating with parents/carers.

Parents/carers (and note that we use these terms synonymously) are vital sources of information to teachers. They can provide important clues which help explain how a child learns or otherwise behaves, and can become 'partners' in supporting their child's educational progress. They hold key information and have a critical role to play in their children's education. This is especially the case if a child has SEN. The Code of Practice (DfEE, 2001) recommends that the parent partnership to meet the educational needs of children with SEN should be based on empowering parents/carers to:

- play an active and valued role in their children's education;
- have difficulties identified early with appropriate intervention to tackle them;
- have a real say in the way in which their child is educated;
- have knowledge of what they can expect for their child as of right; and
- have access to information, advice and support during assessment and any related decision-making process about special educational provision, including transition planning.

This is a very challenging agenda, and it will take time for you to accumulate the skills and the experience necessary to ensure an effective working partnership with parents/carers. It is also likely that your approach will have to vary from parent to parent, based on a sympathetic but professional response to a wide range of concerns that they might have: in other words, try to treat parents/carers – like the children you teach – as individuals! Moreover, we should add another of our words of caution

84

at this point. It is by no means the case that all of your interactions with parents/carers will be 'successful', and result in effective collaboration in the future. It is entirely natural for such relationships to take time to build, and you will find that some parents/carers are more resistant, even hostile to any suggestion of a 'partnership' with teachers. Nonetheless, the continued involvement and support of parents/carers in their child's education is a key factor in helping a classroom teacher to respond to individual learning needs.

There are a number of key principles which can help you to do this, and we would identify three in particular as our underpinning themes in work with parents/carers:

- mutual respect;
- empathy;
- honesty.

Let us briefly examine each of these. Parents/carers have unique insights into the way in which their child responds to learning tasks, social situations, emotions and so on. Teachers need to recognise the value of this information and demonstrate to parents/carers that this 'knowledge' is valuable at each stage of the process of meeting an SEN. It is, for example, very helpful to indicate how you might be able to use information from parents/carers in order to support the child's learning in general or meeting a particular target. Perhaps one of the most obvious ways in which this can be achieved is by placing value on the contribution of parents/carers to a child's IEP. You will find that placing value on what parents/carers themselves bring to a discussion or review of their child's progress will pay rich dividends, either almost immediately or over time. Mutual respect, then, is not something that just happens: it has to be earned.

You need also to place yourself in the position of the parent/carer of the child with SEN. Remember, at the outset, that the parent/carer will most certainly be anxious about what is happening. Some parents/carers, it has been suggested, may experience feelings of embarrassment, guilt or denial about the existence of an SEN (a feeling which takes us back to some of the discussion in the first part of this book). It is also sometimes the case that parents/carers themselves have unhappy memories of their own school days: they may have experienced failure, too – in consequence they may be reluctant to enter into a dialogue with the school. Other parents/carers may view it as solely the teacher's job to deal with SEN; or may see you as an 'authority figure' with whom they have little in common. It is, then, very important that you empathise with these possibilities and seek ways to minimise their impact.

Finally, in our own work with parents/carers – (and we have experienced this as parents/carers ourselves!) – we have always regarded honesty on the part of both teachers and parents/carers as a key component of a successful working partnership. Parents/carers, in our view, recognise the value of explicit, jargon-free accounts by the teacher of a given situation that is affecting their child.

Each of the three underpinning themes outlined above are integral in the way that teachers communicate with parents/carers. This 'front-of-house' style is crucial, in that it creates the initial impression on the parent/carer about what value you place on them as individuals. Once again, the Code of Practice (2001) is very helpful in offering good advice in this respect. It suggests that, in order for communication to be helpful, teachers should:

- recognise the personal and emotional investment of parents and be aware of their feelings;
- focus on the children's strengths as well as areas of additional need;
- ensure that parents/carers understand procedures, are offered support in preparing their contributions and are given documents to be discussed well before meetings;
- respect the validity of differing perspectives and seek constructive ways of reconciling different viewpoints;
- respect the differing needs parents themselves may have, such as a disability or communication barrier; and
- recognise the need for flexibility in the timing and structure of meetings.

Some practical advice about relating to parents/carers would be that you should be:

- non-threatening;
- clear about how parents/carers can help;
- encouraging, while emphasising any additional input that is going to be made.

Ask yourself whether you:

- provide regular opportunities for discussion with parents/carers;
- provide information about their child's progress in ways that are understandable to them and which they can use;
- offer practical ways in which parents/carers can help their children;
- acknowledge the concerns of parents/carers and act constructively upon them;
- are flexible in the timing/location of meetings with parents/carers;
- are blaming the parents/carers for what has happened;
- encourage parents/carers to bring a supportive friend to these meetings.

As you will have noted in Chapter 9, your work as a classroom teacher places a responsibility on you to liaise with parents/carers concerning SEN. Working in partnership with them is a key element of successfully meeting the educational needs of pupils.

Remember too that some schools actively encourage the involvement of parents, often on a rota basis, as classroom helpers. You need to find out what school policy is on this matter in any of your placements. Appendix 11(ii) gives an example of the kind of planning sheet that can assist in making this involvement beneficial for the children – and the teacher!

Finally, it will be useful to know that the SEN Tribunal was set up by the Education Act 1993. It considers parents'/carers' appeals against the decisions of local education authorities (LEAs) about children's SENs, in cases where there is a disagreement between them and the LEA.

www **http://www.dfee.gov.uk/sen/sentrib.htm**

Key reference

Lewis, A. and Capper, L. (2000) 'Converting the reluctant: succeeding with the "hard to reach" parents', *Special Children* **133** (Nov/Dec), 38–9.

This article reports on research into 'Share', a programme devised to foster home–school links, providing useful pointers about working with parents whose children have learning difficulties.

Supporting references

Peck, D. (2000) 'An approach to working with parents of children with language and communication difficulties', *Support for Learning* **15** (4), 172–6.

Wolfendale, S. (1999) 'Parents as Partners in research and evaluation: methodological and ethical issues and solutions', *British Journal of Special Education* **26** (3), 164–9.

Russell, P. (1994) 'The Code of Practice: new partnerships for children with special educational needs', *British Journal of Special Education* **21** (2), 48-52.

Key questions

- What practical benefits can a teacher draw from a positive relationship with the parents/carers of a child with SEN?

- What do you think is the best way of making contact with parents?

- How can teachers best allay the fears that some parents have about coming into school?

School-based task

Write a letter to the parents of a child who has learning difficulties inviting them to discuss their child's progress with you. Discuss this with your school mentor, SENCO or University tutor.

18 Controversial issues

By the end of this chapter you will:

- be familiar with a range of 'controversial' issues concerning SEN;
- be aware of possible sources of additional information.

Like other aspects of education, SEN provision and practice varies in type, focus and meaning. As a result of differences in educational vision, a traditionally strong preoccupation with educational psychology and psychometric measurement, and important social interaction issues like labelling, stereotyping and resultant 'scapegoating' and segregation, SEN is prey to controversy and debate.

You may well encounter such 'controversial issues' during your ITT course – and this will undoubtedly lead to discussion with fellow course members, tutors, school mentors and SENCOs. They include, among others:

- the grouping (or categorisation) of children according to their learning difficulties (as in 'selection');
- the relationships between social and economic disadvantage and SEN;
- race, class and gender issues;
- the use of controlling drugs in behaviour management (e.g. Ritalin);
- the role of the special school;
- the use of invasive therapies (e.g. 'holding therapy' with autistic children);
- the 'reading debate';
- advocacy and self-advocacy and children with SEN.

Because there is such a wide variety of 'controversial issues' it has not been possible to include in-depth coverage of each of these. What we have done therefore, under those issues that we have identified, is to provide a series of questions which can be used in a number of ways. They can help stimulate either group discussion or your own thinking about a topic, and they can act as a reminder to you that very little in education, and not least in SEN, is straightforward and wholly accepted within the teaching profession. You may also want to make use of our questions as focal points for further reading.

The grouping (or categorisation) of children according to their learning difficulties (as in 'selection')

- Is it ethical to group pupils according to their ability?
- How far are these practices contradictory to the principles of inclusive education?
- Is it a practical necessity for classroom teachers to group children by attainment?
- What are some of the likely positive and negative implications for those children who are grouped together as underachievers?

The relationships between social and economic disadvantage and SEN

- In your opinion, is there a causal link between economic disadvantage and SEN?
- Why do some schools have more pupils with learning difficulties than others?
- Should schools that have a high proportion of pupils with SEN be given additional resources/support?
- How can teachers insulate pupils from the educational effects of social and economic disadvantages?

Race, class and gender issues

- Why are boys, rather than girls more frequently identified as having learning difficulties?
- Why has there been an over-representation of black pupils excluded from schools?
- Are teachers culturally alienated from the beliefs and experiences of many of their pupils?
- Should different groups of pupils e.g. boys, be taught in different ways to others?

The use of controlling drugs in behaviour management (e.g. Ritalin)

- Is the use of Ritalin morally defensible?
- Is the use of any drug to control pupil behaviour simply a short-cut measure at the expense of the pupil?
- To what extent is the academic learning of a pupil affected by the use of calming drugs?
- Should teachers and others adults in schools administer drugs?

The role of the special school

- What role do special schools have to play in inclusive education?
- Can a case be made for special schools for certain groups of pupils with SEN and not others?
- Should the curriculum of special schools be different?
- Should all trainee teachers visit a special school as part of their course?

The use of invasive therapies (e.g. 'holding therapy' with autistic children)

- In any education intervention, to what extent do the ends justify the means?
- How far do you believe that the rights of individual children are compromised by interventions that seem to deny choice?
- Should there be some form of 'National kite mark' of intervention strategies used with pupils with SEN?

The 'reading debate'

- What are the positive features of the Literacy Hour that support the pupil with learning difficulties?
- Is literacy presently being assessed in a way which takes account of cultural background of some groups of children?
- Is the preoccupation of measuring literacy compatible with attending to the needs of the underachieving learner?
- Do ITT courses provide sufficient technical background to enable new teachers to enhance children's achievement levels in literacy?

Advocacy and self-advocacy and children with SEN

- To what extent should teachers take account of the views of the learner?
- What happens when the learner's views are in opposition to those of the teacher/school (e.g. as in the case of the pupil regarded as having emotional and behavioural difficulties)?
- Why do you think that there are more advocacy groups involved in supporting some groups (e.g. ASD spectrum) than others (e.g. EBD)?

One issue, which we have not yet mentioned – and yet is so important for all teachers to recognise – is that of child protection. In one sense this is not 'controversial' in that the welfare of children should be the primary concern of all teachers. And yet it is sadly the case that children who have learning difficulties may be more 'at risk' of abuse and exploitation. You should, therefore, be aware of your role in respect of the 1989 Children Act.

www ▪ **http://www.dfee.gov.uk/a-z/CHILD%5FPROTECTION.html**

This gives every child the right to protection from abuse and exploitation and requires that all schools have procedures for handling suspected cases of abuse of pupils. A designated teacher in each school has the responsibility for coordinating action within school and for liaising with other agencies: make sure that you are aware of the identity of this teacher.

The selection of topics and their attended questions in this chapter are simply illustrative of the range of dilemmas and controversies which you will regularly encounter as a practising teacher. The list we have provided is incomplete – for example, we have not mentioned children who are viewed as having Attention Deficit Hyperactivity Disorder (ADHD), or Dyslexic pupils, or children who have challenging behaviours which are organically based (e.g. Tourette's Syndrome) whose behaviour is frequently viewed as antisocial or oppositional. But our list gives you some indication of the range and complexity of controversies that abound in the field of SEN. Given that knowledge is invariably a crucial component of positive action, we encourage you to develop further your understanding of and your critical reflections on each of the above topics.

Key reference

Dyson, A. (1997) 'Social and educational disadvantage: reconnecting special needs education', *British Journal of Special Education* **24** (4), 152–7

Alan Dyson offers a persuasive argument that SEN needs to be viewed more widely than simply a child's school-related difficulties. He suggests that SEN provision on its own is incapable of addressing inequalities both within the education system and in society.

Supporting references

Bush, L. and Hill, T. (1993) 'The right to teach, the right to learn', *British Journal of Special Education* **20** (1), 4–7.
Cooper, P. (1996) 'Giving it a Name: the value of descriptive categories in educational approaches to emotional and behavioural difficulties', *Support for Learning* **11** (4), 146–50.
Garner, P. (2000) ' "Pretzel only policy". Inclusion and the real world of initial teacher education', *British Journal of Special Education* **27** (3), 111–16.
Kniveton, B. H. (1998) 'Underachieving Boys: a Case For Working Harder or Boosting Self Confidence', *Emotional and Behavioural Difficulties* **3** (2), 23–8.
O'Brien, T. (1996) 'Challenging behaviour: Challenging an intervention', *Support for Learning* **11** (4), 162–4.
Parsons, C. and Howlett, K. (1996) 'Permanent exclusions from school: A case where society is failing its children', *Support for Learning* **11** (3), 109–12.

Key questions

- Please refer to those provided in the body of this chapter.

School-based task

Select one of the controversies or dilemmas that we have identified above (or introduce one that we have not highlighted) and invite a teacher colleague to comment on its implications for her practice.

PART FOUR

Developing Your Future Role

In successfully completing your ITT course, and acquiring Qualified Teacher Status (QTS) you have begun what is both a challenging and an exciting journey. No two educational settings, no two pupils or two pieces of their work, will be the same. This in itself will require you to be flexible, open to other's ideas and committed to your own growth as a teacher. Thus, although it will be quite hard for the recently qualified teacher to think in this way, successful completion of an ITT course should be seen as the beginning, rather than the culmination of, your development as a teacher. There is a common saying among experienced teachers that as soon as you stop learning as a teacher then you are in danger of becoming moribund – becalmed as exciting new developments take place around you.

All of this is particularly relevant to SEN, where the rate of change in policy and practice over the last 20 or so years has been dramatic – and is likely to continue in this way for some years to come. Giving serious thought to your own development as a teacher will pay rich dividends in the future – making SEN a focus of such development will be especially beneficial.

19 Planning for professional development

By the end of this chapter you will:

- understand the importance of planning for your professional development in SEN;
- be familiar with the SEN training opportunities available to you and identify a sensible approach to keeping abreast of SEN developments;
- have noted the range of sources of information to assist you in this process.

There are a number of reasons why it is important to make a resolution to keep yourself up to date with what is happening in SEN and inclusion. From a pragmatic point of view it will be essential for you to be aware of any changes that are taking place in the field, so that you can plan for them and incorporate them in your teaching. Moreover, the drive towards more inclusion in schools means that innovation will continue apace – keeping abreast of what is going on will enable you to meet the needs of a wider range of learners in your class.

You will rapidly become aware of the various opportunities open to you to enhance your SEN-related knowledge. These may either be of a more general nature (such as in your LEA NQT induction programme) or highly focused on a particular SEN-related theme (such as a school-based INSET session on IEPs and target setting).

Moreover, you will develop ideas, gather information and extend experience on SEN-related matters by three principal means:

- observation, discussion and reflection around good practice;
- short, one-off courses or training days;
- long courses, leading to a professional award or qualification.

As you begin your teaching career it is likely that you will mainly (though not exclusively) concentrate on the first of these. What you need to do is to develop a system to collate all of the information you acquire. We have found that many of our own students choose to create an SEN file or portfolio, into which they place all related materials. This book can be included as part of this. One useful and easy to manage approach would be to subdivide your collection according to the headings we have adopted in Chapter 2 and 3 of this book: as you obtain a piece of written information on an aspect of SEN you can then place it in the appropriate section. The use of pocket-files for this purpose is ideal: you can make your resources/information even more useful by keeping a regular record of what items you are placing in each pocket-file.

Information on SEN issues can be obtained from a wide variety of sources. These include:

- your school's CPD coordinator or SENCO;
- experienced teacher colleagues;
- your LEA;
- local SEN-related organisations/groups;
- keeping an eye out for publicity for SEN courses or conferences on the staff notice-board;
- checking for articles in the *Times Educational Supplement* and *The Guardian* education pages;
- checking the contents pages of SEN-related journals;
- browsing the web – and especially the sites of SEN-related organisations (see below);
- electronic/distance training opportunities (e.g. New Opportunities Fund (NOF)).

Those with a keen interest in developing their career to encompass some aspect of SEN may even consider joining a national organisation (see the web-sites below), or subscribing to particular professional journals.

It is also becoming more common for new teachers to consider enrolling on an award-bearing course with an SEN focus. We would, however, counsel against rushing into such a course of action. This early stage of your career is mainly about developing a 'plan of action' – and the first stage of this is one of information gathering and of developing a grounding in the basics.

Sources of information – the World Wide Web

In this chapter we will focus explicitly on the World Wide Web (WWW). The SEN resources available through it, combined with the wide range of printed material contained in libraries (including SEN-related journals) will provide a huge amount of useful information.

Before we deal with the WWW, however, let us briefly mention some of the more relevant journals – these we have selected because (a) they relate theoretical issues to practice and (b) they are professional (rather than technical) journals which are readily accessible to teachers. Among those which students tend to find highly pertinent to their work in schools are:

British Journal of Special Education
Educational Psychology in Practice

Emotional and Behavioural Difficulties
Pastoral Care
Special!
Special Children
Support for Learning

In addition, of course, the *Times Educational Supplement* regularly features current issues in SEN, as well as devoting a specific section to it every few months. Gathering relevant news-cuttings from this source is a useful way of adding to your SEN 'file'.

But it is the WWW that is the source of immediate information. All ITT students will be very familiar with its use, although it is unlikely that you will have visited many SEN- or inclusion-specific sites. There is a huge number of these and we list here those which are particularly informative and practically useful. You should also make use of the *links* that these web-sites provide, as well as remembering that other sites are identified elsewhere in this book:

http://www.halcyon.com/marcs/sped.html
A North American Site with a vast range of links.

http://seriweb.com/
Another US site – if you want to survey 'categories' and their continued influence.

http://www.ipsea.org.uk/
This site is specifically focused on offering independent advice to parents.

http://www.sosig.ac.uk/
An excellent general site; click on SEN for some good links.

http://www.basic-skills.co.uk/
A site which, as the name implies, focuses on developing the ability to read and write; other good links.

http://www.nasen.org.uk/
The site of a major SEN-related organisation (The National Association of Special Educational Needs); good links to other sites.

http://www.becta.org.uk/
An excellent site for ICT and SEN; good practical examples.

http://www.canterbury.ac.uk/xplanatory
A very comprehensive site, with excellent links.

http://inclusion.uwe.ac.uk/csie/
The site of the Centre for Studies on Inclusive Education – check its notes for students.

http://www.rnld.co.uk/ie.html
A good site for inclusive education links.

Or email: **awcebd@mistral.co.uk**
The Association of Workers for Children with Emotional and Behavioural Difficulties.

You are encouraged to set up a separate file on your PC which identifies these and other sites as 'favourites'. SEN and inclusion, as we have indicated, are rapidly changing, and you will no doubt want to add other sites as you uncover them.

What access to these various sites, together with a survey of printed matter, will confirm is that SEN and inclusion has been the subject of great attention by theorists, practitioners, policy makers and administrators, all of whom have sought to publicise their viewpoints by various means. So, while you will draw much of sound practical value from these sources, do bear in mind that their writers were, at one point, at a stage of professional development approximating to your own – they were beginning a long, but fruitful process of information gathering. At some stage in the future it is therefore possible that your own reflections could be the subject of articles in journals. Perhaps some of the tasks you have completed in this guide mark the initial steps in this process.

20 Looking to the future

By the end of this chapter you will:

- review what you have covered in this book;
- identify any gaps in your knowledge.

The first thing you might wish to do, as you come close to the end of this book, is to review very briefly the areas you have covered. Use the list below to tick off those areas of SEN/inclusion which you feel you are now a little better informed about. Bear in mind though that you have not reached a point where you can state that you have 'done' SEN: new knowledge, new approaches and new initiatives will mean that you constantly need to update what you know.

We hope you will have:

- gained an understanding of the history of SEN provision;
- explored your own feelings and initial views in relation to SEN;
- developed an awareness of the current context of SEN provision in schools;
- investigated the nature of SEN in your placement school;
- considered the implications of the latest version of the Code of Practice;
- understood your role in SEN as a classroom teacher;
- developed an understanding of some basic strategies to meet pupils' SENs;
- gained insight into the relationship between misbehaviour and SEN;
- become aware of the use and importance of Individual Education Plans;
- found out more about the role of the SENCO;
- become familiar with the content of a school's SEN policy;
- noted the importance of effective relationships with parents/carers;
- explored some of the 'controversial' issues in SEN;
- begun the process of mapping your own professional progression relating to SEN.

Do you see any gaps in your understanding? If so, you can do one or all of several things:

- ask your school mentor, SENCO or course tutor directly about what it is you are unclear about;
- return to the chapter in this book that addresses the issue and review your learning;
- read the specific references provided for the relevant topic of concern;
- discuss the topic with fellow course members.

In the unlikely event that these actions are unsuccessful, you can contact us directly by e-mail. We will be happy to help out.

You can also make use of the proforma provided in Appendix 12, as well as revisiting those contained in Appendix 6. These are simple ways of structuring your thoughts about what you have been able to achieve thus far in respect of SEN involvement, and also help you to see possible areas of weakness which you need to attend to. Critical reflection – which as we have said is built around being honest with yourself (while not being too hard on yourself – and others!) – is the key here.

SEN and inclusion in education are both extremely complex. As you have seen, meeting the learning needs of children who have SEN is a crucial component of educational provision, and it is a statutory requirement that all schools attend to this. By ensuring that SENs are met, schools as a whole benefit. Your ITT course, including its school placements, should give you insights into some of the work in this challenging area. As you embark on, or continue, these studies we conclude by offering the following words of encouragement and advice:

- SEN work is exciting and rewarding.
- Involvement with children who have learning difficulties will enhance your teaching skills.
- Think about the kind of learning experience you provide for these children: do not demean them by thinking that it demands less intensive preparation.
- Many children who have SEN come to regard their 'teacher' as the significant adult in their lives.
- For many your involvement will be perhaps the first time that a significant adult has shown them interest or respect.
- Do not feel upset or concerned if, at first, an SEN child finds it difficult to make progress – remain committed to him – too many have given up on him before.
- Talk with more experienced teachers, look out for opportunities to attend courses.
- Above all, project yourself – be confident, humorous and display an interest in children with learning difficulties. They are often individuals with hidden talents and attributes: seek and you shall find!

We conclude by asking three final questions, and by wishing you good luck and professional fulfilment in your teaching career.

Key questions

- What are your plans to maintain your awareness of SEN/Inclusion issues in your early years of teaching?

- What aspects of SEN/Inclusion are you *really* looking forward to dealing with in your early work as a teacher?

- Where would you look to for guidance and support on an SEN/Inclusion issue at this stage of your career?

Appendix 1

Further reading

Apart from the individual references given in each chapter of this book you are strongly encouraged to seek out other sources. There is now a massive volume of literature on SEN and inclusive education, and you will undoubtedly be given further advice concerning this during the SEN sessions of your teacher training course. In this appendix we provide a summary of some of the books covering each of the topics we have considered in the companion guide as well as books of a more general nature. Where a book has been found to be especially useful by students at *initial training level* we have marked it with an asterisk. You should also access the David Fulton Publishers web-site, which provides a comprehensive set of user-friendly books which will be of direct interest to you.

▐ www ▌ www.fultonpublishers.co.uk

Alban-Metcalfe, J. and Alban-Metcalfe, J. (2001) *Managing Attention Deficit Hyperactivity Disorder in the Inclusive Classroom*. London: David Fulton Publishers.

Armstrong, F. *et al.* (eds) (1999) *Inclusive Education. Policy, Contexts and Comparative Perspectives*. London: David Fulton Publishers.

*Ayers, H. *et al.* (2000) *Perspectives on Behaviour*. London: David Fulton Publishers.

*Babbage, R. *et al.* (1999) *Approaches to Teaching and Learning*. London: David Fulton Publishers.

Balshaw, M. (1999) *Help in the Classroom*. London: David Fulton Publishers.

Benton, P. and O'Brien, T. (2000) *Special Needs and the Beginning Teacher*. London: Continuum.

Beveridge, S. (1999) *Special Educational Needs in Schools*. London: Routledge.

Booth, A. *et al.* (2000) *Index for Inclusion*. Bristol: CSIE. *Special Needs and the Beginning Teacher*. London

Bradley, C. and Roaf, C. (2000) 'Working effectively with LSAs' in P. Benton and T. O'Brien (eds.) *Special Needs and the Beginning Teacher*. London: Cassell

Byers, R. and Rose, R. (2001*) Planning the Curriculum for Pupils with Special Educational Needs*. London: David Fulton Publishers.

Carpenter, B. *et al.* (1996) *Enabling Access*. London: David Fulton Publishers.

Centre for Studies on Inclusive Education (CSIE) (2000) *Index for Inclusion*. Bristol: CSIE.

*Cheminais, R. and Gains, C. (2000) *Special Educational Needs for the Newly Qualified Teacher*. London: David Fulton Publishers.

Clark, C. *et al.* (1995) *Towards Inclusive Schools?* London: David Fulton Publishers.

*Clark, C. *et al.* (1997) *New Directions in Special Needs: Innovations in Mainstream Schools*. London: Cassell.

Clark, C. *et al.* (1998) *Theorising Special Education*. London: Routledge.

Clough, P. (1998) *Managing Inclusive Education: From Policy to Experience*. London: Paul Chapman Publishing.

Cole, T. *et al.* (1998) *Effective Schooling for Pupils with Emotional and Behavioural Difficulties*. London: David Fulton Publishers.

Cooper, P. (1993) *Effective Schools for Disaffected Students*. London: Routledge.

*Cowne, E. (2000) *The SENCO Handbook*. London: David Fulton Publishers.

Cumine, V. *et al.* (1998) *Asperger Syndrome. A Practical Guide for Teachers*. London: David Fulton Publishers.

Daniels, P. and Garner, P. (2000) *The World Yearbook of Education 1999: Inclusive Education*. London: Kogan Page.

*Davies, J. et al. (1998) *Managing Special Needs in the Mainstream School*. London: David Fulton Publishers.

Department of Education and Science (DES) (1989) *The Elton Report*. London: DES.

Derrington, C. et al. (1996) *The Code of Practice: The Impact on Schools and LEAs*. Slough: NFER.

Dyson, A. and Millward, A. (2000) *Schools and Special Needs. Issues of Innovation and Inclusion*. London: Paul Chapman Publishing.

*Farrell, M. (2000) *The Special Education Handbook*. London: David Fulton Publishers.

Farrell, P. (1997) *Teaching Children with Learning Difficulties*. London: Cassell.

Florian, L. et al. (1998) *Prompting Inclusive Practice*. London: Routledge/Falmer.

Garner, P. and Sandow, S. (eds) (1995) *Advocacy, Self Advocacy and Special Needs*. London: David Fulton Publishers.

Garner, P. et al. (1995) *What Teachers do: Developments in Special Education*. London: Paul Chapman Publishing.

*Hornby, G. et al. (1997) *Controversial Issues in Special Education*. London: David Fulton Publishers.

Johnstone, D. (1998) *An Introduction to Disability Studies*. London: David Fulton Publishers.

Jordan, R. (1999) *Autistic Spectrum Disorders. An Introductory Handbook for Practitioners*. London: David Fulton Publishers.

Lacey, P. (2001) *Support Partnerships*. London: David Fulton Publishers.

Lewis, A. (1997) *Special Needs Provision in Mainstream Primary Schools*. London: Routledge.

Long, R. and Fogell, J. (1999) *Supporting Pupils with Emotional Difficulties*. London: David Fulton Publishers.

Lorenz, S. (1998) *Effective In-Class Support*. London: David Fulton Publishers.

McLaughlin, M. and Rouse, M. (eds) (1999) *Special Education and School Reform in the United States and Britain*. London: Routledge.

McNamara, S. and Moreton, G. (1995) *Changing Behaviour*. London: David Fulton Publishers.

*McNamara, S. and Moreton, G. (1997) *Understanding Differentiation*. London: David Fulton Publishers.

*McSherry, J. (2001) *Challenging Behaviours in Mainstream Schools*. London: David Fulton Publishers.

Mittler, P. (2000) *Working Towards Inclusive Education*. London: David Fulton Publishers.

National Curriculum Council (1989) *Curriculum Guidance 2: A Curriculum for All: Special Educational Needs in the National Curriculum*. York: NCC.

National Curriculum Council (1992) *Curriculum Guidance 9: The National Curriculum and Children with Severe Learning Difficulties*. York: NCC.

*O'Brien, T. (1998) *Promoting Positive Behaviour*. London: David Fulton Publishers.

*O'Brien, T. and Guiney, D. (2001) *Differentiation in Teaching and Learning*. London: Continuum.

Parsons, C. (1999) *Education, Exclusion and Citizenship*. London: Routledge.

Porter, G. (1995) 'Organisations of Schooling: achieving access and quality through inclusion'. *Prospects* **25**(7), 299–309.

*Ramjhun, A. (2001) *Implementing the Code of Practice for Children with Special Educational Needs*. London: David Fulton Publishers.

Riddick, B. et al. (2001) *Dyslexia. A Practical Guide for Teachers and Parents*. London: David Fulton Publishers.

Ripley, K. et al. (2001) *Inclusion of Children with Speech and Language Impairments*. London: David Fulton Publishers.

*Roffey, S. and O'Reirdan, T. (1997) *Infant Classroom Behaviour*. London: David Fulton Publishers.

Sandow, S. (ed.) (1994) *Whose Special Need?* London: Paul Chapman Publishing.

Sebba, J. with Sachdev, D. (1997) *What Works in Inclusive Education*. London: Barnardo's.

*Stakes, R. and Hornby, G. (2000) *Meeting Special Needs in Mainstream Schools*. London: David Fulton Publishers.

Thomas, G. and Loxley, A. (2001) *Deconstructing Special Education and Constructing Inclusion*. Buckingham: Open University Press.

Thomas, G. et al. (1998) *The Making of the Inclusive School*. London: Routledge.

Visser, J. and Upton, G. (eds) (1993) *Special Education in Britain after Warnock*. London: David Fulton Publishers.

*Wearmouth, J. (2000) *Special Education Provision*. London: Hodder and Stoughton.

Westwood, P. (1997) *Commonsense Methods for Children with Special Needs*. London: Routledge.

Wolfendale, S. (1997) *Working with Parents/Carers of SEN Children after the Code of Practice*. London: David Fulton Publishers.

Worthington, A. (ed.)(1999) *The Special Education Digest*. London: David Fulton Publishers.

Appendix 2

SEN timeline

1894   **New Education Act for blind and deaf**

1899   **Elementary Education (Defective and Epileptic Children) Act**

1921   **Education Act**
- Recognised five categories – blind, deaf, mentally defective, physically defective, epileptic)

1937   **Education (Deaf Children) Act**

1944   **Education Act**
- Education according to age, aptitude and ability
- Special education can take place in mainstream as well as in special schools

           Special education regulations
- Identified 10 categories of need

1955   **Underwood Report**
- Identified need for provision for maladjusted children
- Need for child guidance service

1970   **Education (Mentally Handicapped Children) Act**
Responsibility for severely subnormal moved from NHS to LEA

1973   **Circular 4/73**
Recommended small classes for handicapped pupils

1976   **Education Act**
Section 10 – integration of all handicapped pupils to be introduced

1978   **Warnock Report**
- Coined the term SEN
- SEN to include 20 per cent of school population
- Abolition of statutory categories
- Multi-professional assessment
- Focus on individual educational needs
- Consultation with parents
- Emphasis on additional in-service training in SEN

1981   **Education Act**
- Many Warnock recommendations translated into legislation
- Statementing procedure introduced
- Multi-agency involvement in assessment process

1983   **Education Act enforced**

1988   **Education Act**
   • Introduction of the National Curriculum
   • Entitlement to a broad/balanced curriculum

1989   **United Nations Convention on the Rights of the Child**

1989   **Children Act**
   • Participation of children in decision making

1989   **The Elton Report** (on Discipline in Schools)

1993   **Education Act (Section 3: Code of Practice for the Identification and Assessment of Pupils with Special Educational Needs)**
   • Guidance for staged process of classroom and external support
   • SENCO in every school
   • SEN policy in every school
   • IEPs to be written
   • SEN Tribunal

1994   **Circular 6/94 Regulations on Special Educational Provision**

1994   **Circular 8/94 Pupil Behaviour and Discipline**

1994   **Circular 9/94 The Education of Children with Emotional and Behavioural Difficulties**

1995   **Circular 10/94 The Education of Children with Emotional and Behavioural Difficulties**

1996   **Education Act** (Section 550A) **The Use of Force and Control to Restrain Pupils** (Enforced in September 1998)

1997   **DfEE Excellence for All Children: meeting special educational needs (Green Paper)**
   • Planned goals for provision by 2002

1998   **TTA National Standards for SENCOs**

1998   **Circular 1/98 Behaviour Support Plans**

1999   **DfEE Meeting Special Educational needs: A programme of action**
   • Working with parents
   • Developing an SEN framework
   • More inclusive education system
   • Developing knowledge and skills
   • Working in partnership

1999   **National SEN Specialist Standards**

1999   **National Numeracy Strategy**

2000   **National Literacy Strategy**

2000   **SEN and Disability Rights Bill (for consultation)**

2000   **Draft Revised Code of Practice**

2000   **DfEE Working with Teaching Assistants: a good practice guide**

2000   **TTA National Special Educational Needs Specialist Standards**

2000   **Special educational Needs and Disability Bill**
   • Disability Rights Commission to prepare new Code of Practice to explain legislation on the discrimination provisions for education providers, disabled people and others

2001   **Introduction of the Connexions Service**

2002   **DfEE Revised Code of Practice introduced**

Appendix 3

The Warnock Report /1981 Education Act (Summary)

This Act was substantially based on the findings of the Warnock Report (1978). It covers:

- Definition of SEN and the 'end' of categorisation
- Mainstream schooling for children with learning difficulties
- Statementing process (five-stage)
- Parental involvement
- LEA responsibilities
- Procedures for identifying and assessing children.

The 1981 Education Act defined Special Educational Needs as follows:

1. For the purposes of this Act a child has special educational needs if he has a learning difficulty which calls for special educational provision to be made for him.

2. Subject to subsection (4) ... a child has a learning difficulty if:
    (a) he has a significantly greater difficulty in learning than the majority of children of his age;
    (b) he has a disability which either prevents or hinders him from making use of educational facilities of a kind generally provided in schools within the area of the local authority concerned, for children of his age;
    (c) he is under the age of five years, and is, or would be if special educational provision were not made for him, likely to fall within paragraph (a) or (b) when over that age.

3. Special educational provision means:
    (a) in relation to a child who has attained the age of two years, educational provision which is additional to or different from the educational provision made generally for children of his age in schools maintained by the local education authority concerned.
    (b) in relation to any child under that age, educational provision of any kind.

Appendix 4

The Code of Practice (1994): key features

i. The 'stages' of assessment and intervention

A five-stage process followed what had become good practice in a range of LEAs, and operates as follows:

Stage 1:   Class or subject teachers identify or register a child's special educational needs and with the consulting SENCO, take initial action. This may involve adapting or changing curricular materials, changing the child's position in the classroom or otherwise providing some differentiation.

Stage 2:   If this does not deal with the problem, the SENCO takes the lead responsibility for gathering information and for coordinating provision.

Stage 3:   Teachers and SENCO are supported by external specialists (educational psychologist, therapist, etc.).

Stage 4:   LEA considers the need for statutory assessment and if appropriate makes a multidisciplinary assessment.

Stage 5:   LEA considers whether to make a statement of SEN and if one is made, arranges, monitors and reviews the special provision. This may involve the engagement of support staff, or the purchase of special equipment.

At all stages, parents/carers should be kept informed of the situation, and their help sought in devising the programme for the child. Liaising with the parents/carers is primarily the responsibility of the SENCO, but will also involve the class teacher.

At Stage 2, the SENCO should draw up an Individual Education Plan (IEP), comprising:

- nature of the child's difficulties;
- action to be taken including: special provision, staff involved, including frequency of support, specific programmes/activities/equipment;
- help from parents/carers at home;
- targets to be achieved in a given time;
- pastoral care or medical requirements;
- monitoring and assessment arrangements;
- review arrangements and date.

This process is most likely to take place in the primary school, but sometimes it may begin in the secondary school.

ii. School SEN policies

In addition, the Code of Practice states that:

Schools must publish the policy details regarding special educational needs. (2.10).

This must include:

- basic information about the policy;
- information about the school's policies for identification assessment and provision;
- information about the school's staffing policies and external partnerships;
- an annual report about the implementation of these policies.

iii. The role of the SENCO

From 1994 every school now had to appoint a member of staff as Special Educational Needs Coordinator (SENCO). Specifically, the SENCO is responsible for:

- day-to-day management of SEN policy;
- liaising with and advising fellow teachers;
- coordinating provision for SEN;
- maintaining the SEN register and overseeing records;
- liaising with parents/carers of children with SEN;
- contributing to INSET;
- liaising with external agencies.

iv. The Individual Education Plan (IEP)

An individual education plan (IEP) is a planning document which describes a pupil's short-term learning needs and the arrangements made to monitor and review needs and provision.
   To start with, the teacher may be asked to provide:

- a record of her observations;
- curriculum assessments;
- National Curriculum levels;
- individual assessments, perhaps from subject teachers;
- records of emotional and behavioural difficulties;
- concentration levels and distractibility;
- positive aspects of the pupil's performance.

Good record keeping is essential, for nothing can begin without it! Successful target setting requires a sound assessment of a pupil's learning needs. Targets need to be *clear, realistic, precise*, and *agreed* with the pupil. All those involved need to know what is required of them, and finally dates for review need to be set with all those involved.

Appendix 5

The Revised Code of Practice

PROPOSALS (as of July, 2001) include:

GUIDANCE FOR SCHOOLS AND SCHOOL-BASED STAGES OF THE CODE

Flexibility

Emphasising the fact that the Code is to be interpreted in the light of the individual school's circumstances.

Secondary schools

Provide more guidance as to how secondary schools can meet the statutory SEN responsibilities and provide guidance on setting targets and monitoring progress. A separate Code for primary and secondary schools will not be produced.

SEN Coordination (SENCOs)

Guidance on the time that might be required for SEN Coordination.

Teachers Green Paper and TTA standards

Reflect the outcomes of the Teachers Green Paper and refer to the TTA standards.

Under fives

Extend the present guidance on the assessment and statements for children under five and incorporate existing guidance provided for private nurseries and other under-five providers.

IEPs

Include models of IEP formats and emphasise the value of concise IEPs, focused on three or four targets.

Stages of the Code

Reduce the school-based stages to two (*School Support* and *Support Plus*). Parental access to statutory assessment at Stage 4 and the legal protection offered by a statement will **not** be constrained.

Develop guidance on the procedures for Statutory Assessment and Statements and clarify that there should be no routine expectation of progression to Stage 4.

Provide guidance on the kind of monitoring, provision and information for parents appropriate at a 'pre-Code' stage.

Emphasise the need for regular assessment and monitoring of children under *School Support* and *Support Plus*.

Emphasise the need for schools to consider whether a child progresses to a further stage or should be removed from the SEN register.

Develop a different term to describe the elements of the Code, since the present term 'stages' implies an upward progression through the stages.

Children whose first language is not English	More guidance on the identification and assessment of children whose first language is not English and who may have SEN.
Parent Partnership Services	Extend guidance on the role and function expected of local parent partnership services.
	Provide guidance on the role of Independent Parental Supporters similar to that offered at present by Named Persons.
	Remove the current obligation on LEAs to provide parents with a Named Person.

ASSESSMENT

Criteria for making statutory assessment	Rationalise the present guidance and include reference to Autism.
Child's views	Strengthen the existing guidance to encourage LEAs and schools to seek and take account of the child's views throughout the SEN process.
Appeals to the SEN Tribunal	Amend the Act to allow appeals from parents or from schools or other agencies (at present appeals can only be made by parents) and require LEAs to consider requests from a school or other agencies (as well as parents) and to make a decision within six weeks.
	Provide examples of good practice in the area of conciliation arrangements which can help resolve disagreements with parents to prevent appeals.
	Provide an annex setting out the basis on which appeals to the Tribunal may be made.
	Provide guidance on reasonable timescales for implementing Tribunal orders.
Medical conditions	Omit the present list of medical conditions included in the Code, since some LEAs and schools are interpreting this to imply that a child with any of the specified conditions should automatically be given a statement, and a child who does not have one or more of these conditions should not be given a statement.
Benefits	Include a recommendation that LEAs should advise parents to check with social services, parent support groups or voluntary bodies, to see if they may be entitled to further benefits.

STATEMENTS

Lists of schools	Amend the Notice to Parents to exclude the long list of non-maintained and independent schools (most of which are not local) and replace it with a statement to advise parents that they may, if they wish, apply to the LEA for copies.
Transport	Clarify that the statement referring to the provision of transport for children with a statement is a 'non-educational provision'.
Speech and language therapy	Review and revise the terms in which SLT provision should be described, in light of the difficulties experienced by LEAs to provide this support sufficient to meet the needs of children with or without a statement.
Childcare	Consider whether changes to the Code are necessary in light of the National Childcare Strategy.

Financial arrangements for parents seeking independent school placement	Modify the 'model statement' in the Schedule to the 1994 SEN Regulations to include the possibility of a reference to 'any special financial arrangements pertaining to the child's placement'.
Delegation of funds for provision in statements	Extend guidance to reflect that the LEA cannot delegate its duty to secure that all the provision specified in the statement is made and in the event of an agreement by a school to meet such provision breaking down, the LEA will be expected to ensure that the provision is made.

ANNUAL REVIEWS OF STATEMENTS, TRANSITIONAL REVIEWS

Reduced paperwork	Opportunities will be explored to reduce the paperwork required of schools and LEAs in relation to annual reviews.
Transitional reviews	Strengthen existing guidance and amend Regulations to:

> replace the current statutory requirement for a transitional annual review at the age of 14+ with a requirement for an annual review during year 9;
>
> require schools to play the same role for transitional reviews as for other annual reviews;
>
> clarify the procedures for annual reviews subsequent to the transitional review;
>
> amend legislation for pupils with SLD or PMLD to enable LEAs to postpone transitional reviews to Year 10 or 11.

Transfer between phases	Ensure that that statements are amended early enough in the transfer procedure to give parents opportunity to appeal to the SEN Tribunal and for the appeal to be resolved before the start of the next school year. Such reviews of statements will need to be completed by 31 December of the preceding year and consequent amendments made by 15 February.
EP involvement	Revisions will be made to reflect the outcomes of consultation on the future role of EPs. These are likely to include clarification that EPs do not necessarily have to attend annual reviews.
Supported employment	Inclusion of a statement to the effect that one option for consideration at the transition review is supported employment at 16,18 or later and that a representative of supported employment be invited to future transition review meetings.
Ceasing to maintain a statement	More detailed guidance to be included in the Code regarding the LEA's responsibility for ceasing to maintain a statement.

USER FRIENDLINESS

Location of index	An index to be placed at the very end of the Revised Code.
Notice to parents	Amendments to make the Notice more accessible to parents.
Layout and design	Enhancing the accessibility of the Code e.g. use of colour-coding for different chapters.
Order of chapters	Review of the ordering of chapters e.g. the chapter on Under fives to come earlier.
Form of presentation	Hard copy and CD-Rom versions to be available via the DfEE SEN site of the National Grid.

(Adapted from SENCO Update: supporting special education needs coordinators. Autumn 2000.)

Appendix 6(i)

Reflecting on your initial/subsequent school placements

(Completing each of the sections at an early stage of your ITT course will provide useful baseline data for you. Compare it with some of your later observations – see over.)

- What did you see which immediately 'got you thinking' about the different ways in which children learn and behave ?

- What information did you uncover about the range of learning needs in the school?

- How did it impact on the way that the teachers did their job?

- What are your recollections of a single SEN issue arising from a lesson you observed?

- How did children with SENs respond to you?

- Did you identify specific characteristics in the way that SEN provision was organised?

- What advice did you gather about SEN from other teachers? The SENCO?

- Have your views regarding SEN changed in any way as a result of this experience?

SEN: reflecting on your subsequent school placement(s)

(Compare your responses to each of the sections below with those you made earlier in your ITT course. Can you detect any significant differences? What might be the reasons behind these?)

- What did you see which immediately 'got you thinking' about the different ways in which children learn and behave?

- What information did you uncover about the range of learning needs in the school?

- How did it impact on the way that the teachers did their job?

- What are your recollections of a single SEN issue arising from a lesson you observed?

- How did children with SENs respond to you?

- Did you identify specific characteristics in the way that SEN provision was organised?

- What advice did you gather about SEN from other teachers? The SENCO?

- Have your views regarding SEN changed in any way as a result of this experience?

Appendix 6(ii)

Guidance on easing your way into classroom life

A starting point in understanding the nature of a child's learning difficulties, as well as dealing with your own feelings about SEN, is to familiarise yourself with the child, both as an individual and as a member of a larger group or whole class. Quite apart from going some way to ensuring that you don't see the 'SEN' as being the only characteristic of the child, it will enable you to begin the process of building up trust and confidence in the child. The following advice is applicable to all children, of course – but as you read it try to keep the pupil who has a learning difficulty at the forefront of your thinking.

You may initially feel apprehensive, but a good way to relax and ease your way into classroom life is to show an interest in individual children or the activities of small groups. Chat to the children informally – hopefully your appreciation of what they are doing and your respect for them as people will be genuine! If so, they should respond with friendliness and trust. You don't want to appear 'distant' to the children – avoid being too formal and brisk and don't become a detached 'onlooker'.

Try to:

- become familiar with the children's names straight away. Children will respond well if you call them by name. You will be more readily accepted as part of their lives in school/nursery. Make sure they also know your name – if you can do this informally they will probably find you more approachable;
- treat the children as the unique individuals they are; you will quickly come to appreciate the differences between them;
- appreciate the reasons children have for their actions. In doing so, attempt to see things from their point of view as well as your own;
- be consistent – avoid 'going back' on what you say to a child;
- talk in positive rather than negative terms, e.g. 'Speak one at a time, then we can hear what everyone has to say', rather than, 'Don't all shout out at once';
- remember that it is not only what you say which communicates messages to children. Your facial expressions and gestures are significant. Children will find meaning in everything you do and will respond well to signs that you respect both themselves and the work they do. Respect the efforts of all children, not just the 'fastest' and 'best';
- think about practical matters such as access to materials, cleaning up, movement around the classroom, the need to supervise the whole class when working with one group, making sure children have heard what is being said, etc. and work out ways of developing organisation ability;
- spend time talking with the children. Use any opportunities you can to do this. Conversations can occur in all sorts of situations – some when children are focusing on a learning activity; others at the beginnings or ends of sessions or during playtimes, etc. Children often like to talk about things they have brought into school or things that they've been doing outside school. Try to make a mental note of how the conversations get started and how they develop. What thoughts go through your mind as you are having these conversations?
- use any opportunities you can to find out about children's personal worlds. Avoid prying by asking specific questions, but tune into what children tell you about their own experiences, thoughts and feelings. If you are having conversations with the children, this shouldn't be difficult. Here are some things to be thinking about:

How do they see their home, family, friends, school/nursery and neighbourhood?

How do they feel about things (their hopes and fears, their interests)?

What sense do they give to the world around them?

What is important to them?

What kind of things do they spend their time doing?

What is it like being a child in school today? No doubt you'll be making comparisons with your own experience as a child.

Observe the children closely. Think about what you notice. What does it mean? What does it tell you?

(Adapted from © NTU BA (Hons) QTS Year 1 Handbook 2000/2001.)

Examples of Individual Education Plans (Primary and Secondary)

City of NOTTINGHAM

Education Department

INDIVIDUAL EDUCATION PLAN

Date: April 2000	IEP No: 4

PUPIL INFORMATION

Name of child/young person: Lauren

DOB: 2/4/93	Stage: 2
Class: 5	Year Group: 2

AREA(S) OF NEED

- General learning delay
- Poor social skills
- Delayed expressive language

TARGET	SUPPORT STRATEGIES	REVIEW
To successfully take a simple message to another teacher	Teacher to ensure regular opportunities – Lauren to be accompanied by peer	Achieved – Lauren now to deliver message on own
To indicate the first word on the page	Teacher to model during shared and guided reading	Achieved – able to demonstrate on big book during shared text work
To identify and name characters from the Oxford Reading Tree	Work on Oxford Reading Tree Level 1 during guided reading (with LSA 3 x 15 mins per week) and during independent literacy hour work	Ongoing – can name 4 out of 6 – still to learn Biff and Flipper
To count objects accurately to 5	During 5–10 minutes oral/mental calculation work in Daily Maths Lesson	Achieved – now focusing on 6, 7, 8
To recognise numbers 1, 2, 3	As above	Achieved – Focusing on 3, 4
To write 1 and 2 independently		Ongoing – reversing 2
To take part in a small group acitivity and take turns	During supported small group work in Daily Maths Lesson (2 x 20 mins weekly)	Ongoing – still needs prompting when it is her turn
	Teacher/LSA to encourage during small group work in LH and DML	

Parental involvement:	Additional information/further action required	Staff involved:
Mum to meet class teacher briefly once a week		Class teacher
Will share a book every night		LSA for small group work – 1 hour 25 mins weekly (school support)
		Next Review: July 2000

116

INDIVIDUAL EDUCATION PLAN

City of NOTTINGHAM

Education Department

Date: April 2000	IEP No: 3

PUPIL INFORMATION

Names:	Stage:	Year Group:	Class	DOB:
Abdul	2	3	1	7/12/91
Joe	2	3	2	3/5/92
Alisa	2	3	1	11/6/92
Jenny	2	3	2	26/1/92

AREA(S) OF NEED:
- *End of Year 2 screening identified gaps in phonological awareness*
- *Unable to discriminate, blend and spell initial consonant clusters from Year 1, term 2 phonic list*
- *Poor cursive script, incorrect letter formation. Not yet joining*

TARGET	SUPPORT STRATEGIES	REVIEW
• *To hear, say and recognise set of ten initial consonant clusters: cl ch cr th tr thr dr dw fl fr*	• *Over 5 weeks – small group LSA support with literacy hour (2 x 20 minute sessions weekly)*	• *although targets linked directly to children's need there were too many clusters to learn over the 5 week block*
• *To form same set of 10 initial consonant clusters correctly*	• *use recognised handwriting scheme, focusing on 2 clusters per week* – *game (to hear, say and recognise)* – *activity sheet (to practise formation and then join)*	• *group confident with cl ch cr th tr thr clusters – need to spend additional 2 weeks on dr dw fl fr*
• *To form same set of 10 initial consonant clusters*	• *at end of 5 week block assess to check understanding*	• *all children can form letters correctly but Alisa struggled with basic joins – use independent work in literacy hour to support this*
		• *Next step – set targets for next half term, focusing on initial clusters not covered and introduction to end clusters*

Parental involvement: • *Parents informed through individual letter* • *Abdul's father met LSA and had opportunity to look at resources*	Additional information/further action required N/A	**Staff involved:** Class teacher LSA: 20 mins x 2 weekly (school support) Next Review: July 2000

Appendix 8

Example of a school's SEN policy

WESTLAND PRIMARY SCHOOL

Westland Primary School has approximately 78 pupils divided into three classes (numbers may fluctuate annually).

Class 1 – R and Y1
Class 2 – Y2 and Y3
Class 3 – Y4, Y5 and Y6

Children come from Westland village or the local area – see the Admissions policy.

This policy has been produced by the Governors and Staff of Westland Primary School, following participation of the SENCO in the Code of Practice organised by the LEA.

Aims

We aim to provide the atmosphere in which all children can reach their full potential, where the individual needs of all children are met, valued and understood. All children are of equal worth and have equal opportunities.

SEN Coordinator: Mrs L. Walker

The SEN coordinator is responsible for:

a) the day-to-day operation of the school's SEN policy;
b) liaising with and advising class teachers;
c) coordinating with the Head in managing the provision for pupils with SEN;
d) updating and overseeing the records of all pupils with SEN;
e) maintaining the register, action taken and outcomes;
f) working with parents of children with SEN;
g) liaising with external agencies including the Educational Psychology Service and other support agencies, medical and social services and voluntary bodies;
h) contributing to INSET training for all staff;
i) attending review meetings of SEN pupils and statemented pupils where appropriate.

Admission arrangements

Children begin school on a part-time basis in the Reception class. They only commence full-time education when it is considered to be appropriate by the staff and parents working in consultation. Individual programmes will be made for any child with special educational needs.

The school building prevents children who are severely handicapped by physical disability from attending Westland Primary School. Many steps and stairs would be a safety hazard for a wheel-chair pupil. Ramps cannot be built at the side of the school due to the severity of the incline. The DT area downstairs is available for pupils to work in small groups.

The SEN register is checked regularly.

Definition of SEN

A child has special educational needs if he or she has a learning disability, which calls for special educational provision to be made for her or him.

A child has a learning difficulty if he or she:

- has significantly greater difficulty in learning than the majority of children of the same age.

Special educational provision means provision which is additional to, or different from, the educational provision generally available in LEA schools. About 20 per cent of children will exhibit special educational needs at some time in their school career. The confidentiality of the child must be respected.

The responsibilities of the Governing Body

The governing body should have regard for the Code of Practice when carrying out duties towards all children with SEN.

They should ensure that the necessary provision is made for pupils with SEN.

In cooperation with the Head teacher and SENCO, they should determine the school's general policy and approach to provision for children with SEN.

They should ensure that the teachers are aware of the importance of identifying and providing for those children with SEN.

They should report annually to parents on the success of the school's policy for pupils with SEN to include information about identification, assessment, provision, monitoring and record keeping and use of outside agencies and services.

A current update of SEN should be reported at each Governors' meeting.

A report on the number of SEN children at each stage and any significant change in policy should be given in consultation with the LEA and other schools.

They should ensure that pupils with special educational needs are integrated as far as possible into the activities of the school and with other children.

They should consult with the LEA and the governing bodies of other schools, when appropriate, in the interests of coordinated SEN provision in the area.

Miss C. Stevens is the SEN nominated Governor for the school.

Objectives

a) to meet the individual needs of all children irrespective of whether they have physical, sensory, emotional, behavioural, specific or general learning needs. In particular to be aware of the standards of achievement of individual pupils in reaching their educational needs.

b) to promote continuity of approach through step-by-step attention to individual needs;

c) to satisfy the requirements of the 1993 Education Act by giving all children the entitlement to a broad, balanced, relevant and differentiated education. Modification of and disapplication from the National Curriculum, will only be undertaken in exceptional circumstances and only if this is in the best interest of the pupil;

d) to provide appropriate resources, both human and material, and to ensure their maximum and proper use;

e) to involve the child in the process of identification, assessment and provision and to ensure that the child is aware that his or her wishes will be taken into account as part of the process and of the shared responsibility in meeting his or her educational needs;

f) to promote the successful integration of children with special educational needs into mainstream school;

g) to involve parents at an early stage, to develop a home/school partnership working together for the benefit of the child.

The process of identification assessment of SEN

a) observation of the classroom and playground by teacher and LSW to note areas of concern or lack of maturity. Close contact with parents should be developed and any preschool information should be used;

b) the initial reception baseline assessments will be completed by Autumn half-term and the end of reception assessments by July of each year;

c) MIST (a standardised test – Middle Infant Screening Test) will be used with appropriate Y1 pupils and this will identify future learning needs;

d) SATS will be completed by Y2 children (as well as Y6 children) and NFER reading tests by Y3 and Y5 children;

e) a sight or hearing test may be requested at any time by any member of staff.

If at any time there is any cause for concern about any aspect of the child's development, the class teacher should inform the SENCO and a programme of support devised.

Causes for concern can be identified by the class teacher, non-teaching assistants, mid-day supervisors, parents or outside agencies.

It is important that assessments are diagnostic to identify needs and help to plan a programme of support.

Provision for SEN

a) In class R/Y1 the LSW is able to give extra support in helping children to overcome short-term difficulties.

b) Children are withdrawn from their classes to work in small groups with the SENCO on Wednesday and Thursday mornings. Parents are asked to support and reinforce their activities.

The school-based stages of assessments

Stage 1

A child who is finding it harder to learn than his/her peers or has a disability. The class teacher reviews the teaching strategies with the SENCO.

The SENCO talks with the parents.

The child's progress is monitored and reviewed at an agreed date.

Review

The child continues under Stage 1 with further reviews.

The child no longer needs special differential help.

If after two reviews the child has not made satisfactory progress then move to Stage 2.

Stage 2

A child reaches Stage 2 if he/she fails to respond to the teaching strategies worked out for him/her at Stage 1.

Criteria: R.A. below C.A.
Below average SAT's scores
Showing concern on baseline assessment
MIST screening in Y1
Disability holding him/her back from progress

The SENCO is responsible for coordinating the child's special educational provision in conjunction with parents and teachers. The coordinator gathers information and produces an individual education plan (IEP) including:

a) nature of the child's learning difficulties with precise curriculum priorities;
b) special educational provision, size of group, frequency and timing of support;
c) involvement of staff in specific programme, activities, materials, equipment and teaching strategies;
d) non-curricular needs, pastoral care and medical requirements;
e) informs and enlists help from parents;
f) targets to be achieved over a given time and criteria for success;
g) any additional support arrangements;
h) date for review and those involved.

Review

This is carried out by the SENCO in consultation with the class teacher and the parent and focuses on progress, effectiveness of the plan, contribution from parents, updated information and future action.

a) Child continues at Stage 2, with further targets in a revised IEP and subsequent reviews.
b) Child reverts to Stage 1 or no longer requires help but remains on the SEN register until it is clear that the child's progress does no cause concern.
c) Child moves to Stage 3 if outside agencies need to be involved.

Stage 3

The school calls upon external specialised support (psychologists, learning support service, specialists in sensory impairment, health or social services). The parents and the child should be kept informed.

Reports and advice from the experts should be collected. An IEP should be written, setting out the strategies for support and monitoring in liaison with specialists.

Review

The child continues at Stage 3 with further targets and reviews.

The child reverts to Stage 2 or 1 with action and support appropriate to those stages within the school SEN arrangements.

The child is referred to the LEA for Statutory Assessment under Stage 4, if progress is not satisfactory.

Stage 4

When the child is referred, the following should be available:

a) written information on educational and other assessments and reports from outside agencies;
b) views of the parents and child;
c) information on the child's health and any Social Services or EWO involvement;
d) written evidence of the school's action under the first three stages;
e) education plans for the child;
f) reports and reviews and their outcomes;
g) reports of involvement of other professionals.

The school may consider disapplying the National Curriculum at this stage.

The LEA considers the need for a Statutory Assessment, and, if appropriate, makes a multi-disciplinary assessment in cooperation with the school, parents and other agencies.

Stage 5

The LEA considers the need for a statement and, if appropriate, makes a statement, arranges and monitors and reviews the provision. Parents must be given a draft of the proposed statement, and the parents may make representation, which the LEA must consider, before issuing the final statement. This statement must be reviewed annually and be attended by an LEA representative, child's parents, by the SENCO and a relevant teacher. Other professionals may be invited. The outcome of the review may be to amend the existing statement, amend the provision, amend the placement or cease to maintain the statement.

Appeals

A regional SEN Tribunal will enable the parents to appeal on any of the following issues:

LEA refusal to make a statement
Contents of the statement
LEA refusal to make a statutory assessment
LEA refusal to reassess a child who already has a statement
LEA decision to maintain a statement
LEA decision not to change the name of the school offered in the statement

The decision of the SEN Tribunal will be binding on the LEA and there will be no further stage of appeal unless a parent takes up a point of law or judicial procedure.

The more able child

The school will at all times endeavour to be aware of and satisfy the needs of the more able child by:

a) matching tasks to abilities;
b) providing educational opportunity commensurate to ability;
c) a particularly gifted child will be referred to external specialised supporters (e.g. psychologist, learning support services, LEA, etc.).

Provision

The provision must be flexible and relevant to the needs of the child and promote self-esteem.

Withdrawal must not jeopardise the child's right to a broad and balanced curriculum.

Staffing and qualifications

Veronica Lee: Head teacher. BA MEd Teacher Q.T. status. Experience in teaching special needs class and English as a second language.

Elizabeth Shearer: B.Ed. SENCO Teacher Q.T. status. Experience in teaching special needs. SENCO at previous school.

Jacqueline Rutter: BA PGCE Teacher Q.T. status. Experience in working with special needs unit at previous school.

Patricia Wallace: LSW Cert 3211 City and Guilds. Experience in working with special needs children.

Susan Holland: LSW Cert 3211 City and Guilds. Experience in working with special needs children.

Ann Gardiner: LSW. Experience in working with special needs children.

Parents and friends of the school come in at regular intervals to work with small groups of children or individuals, to hear reading and help with games, painting and other topic work. Parents of children receiving special help ensure that their child does any homework required and brings it back to school.

Educational Psychologist consulted and advice followed for children with autism and behavioural problems.

Hearing impaired service monitor and advise suitable strategies for helping children with hearing problems.

SEN advisory service monitor, and advice given to learning difficulties.

School doctor consulted about any health problems.

Appendix 9

Example of a SENCO's job description

WESTLAND COUNTY PRIMARY SCHOOL JOB DESCRIPTION

Post: Assistant Teacher
Holder: Mrs R. Smith   **Grade:** Mainscale Point 9

Relationships

Mrs Smith is responsible to the Head Teacher for her teaching duties, tasks and responsibilities, and for the supervision of the work of the Nursery Assistant.

Mrs. Smith interacts on a professional level with colleagues and seeks to establish and maintain productive relationships with them in order to promote mutual understanding of subjects in the school curriculum, with the aim of improving the quality of teaching and learning in the school.

Purpose of the job

To undertake the teaching of general subjects to a Reception/Year 1 class and pastoral and administrative duties in respect of pupils in this class, as well as the responsibilities in the school as agreed with the Head Teacher.

Key tasks

1. To teach general subjects as agreed with the Head Teacher to pupils in a Key Stage 1 class and participate in the development of schemes of work, materials and syllabuses for such subjects, and attend meetings on such matters, as required.
2. To control and oversee the use and storage of books, stationery and other teaching materials related to her teaching, ensuring that any Health and Safety Regulations are observed.
3. To carry out the duties of a class teacher in respect of pupils, including:
   a) the maintenance of discipline and acceptable standards of conduct and appearance of pupils;
   b) the establishment of a rapport with pupils to develop their social and academic potential and to be a part-time source of reference for their problems;
   c) making records and reports on the personal and social needs of the pupils and assessing, recording and reporting on the development, progress and attainments of pupils in each case having regard for the curriculum for the school;
   d) the undertaking of any other administrative duties in respect of her class as required by the Head Teacher;
   e) the setting and marking of homework for pupils if necessary or appropriate;
   f) playing a part in assemblies by escorting pupils to and from assemblies and attending staff meetings as required.

4. To supervise the work of the Nursery Assistant appropriate to her class. To carry out supervision of pupils as detailed by the Head Teacher.
5. To participate as required in meetings with colleagues, other professionals and parents in respect of the duties and responsibilities of the post.

6. To keep abreast of trends and developments in education, especially those relevant to the duties and responsibilities of the post.

To undertake the role of SENCO as follows:

To identify with the class teacher any child needing special needs help. To assess these children to ascertain the level and stage of help needed.

To communicate with the parents of each special needs child to keep them up-to-date with their child's progress and to ensure their involvement at all stages.

To draw up, monitor, record and evaluate programmes of work at appropriate levels for children receiving special needs help (Individual Education Plans – IEPs).

To liaise with outside support agencies e.g. Educational Psychologist where appropriate for the child needing extensive support.

To attend review meetings of special needs and statemented children where appropriate. Reporting to the Head Teacher or direct to the Governors about the special needs work being undertaken in the school.

Having curriculum responsibilities for Maths and Music involving:

Attending relevant courses and disseminating information to all the staff.

Organising the Maths and Music curricula within the school and ensuring National Curriculum requirements are met.

Suggesting appropriate resources for carrying out the Maths and Music curricula within the school.

Being able to work alongside members of staff needing help by offering relevant information appertaining to the Maths and Music activity to be undertaken, suggesting ways and means of carrying this out, evaluating and appraising the results.

Organising INSET days and staff meetings as and when necessary relating to the Maths and Music curricula.

Informing the Governors, if necessary, of any new initiatives undertaken by the school relating to the Maths and Music curricula.

The duties and responsibilities of the post are subject to those detailed in the National Statement of Conditions of Employment and will count as directed time as detailed in that statement, and as defined by the Head Teacher.

This job description does not define in detail all the duties/responsibilities of the post, and will be reviewed at least once a year and may be subject to modification or amendment after consultation and agreement with the post holder.

September 2000

Mrs Rebecca Smith
Contract: Full-time hours: 1265
938 hours 15 minutes – direct contact time with pupils and attendance at
in-service days.

22 hours 30 minutes – contact with parents as regards SEN needs.

85 hours 30 minutes – 15 minutes before start of the morning session and 15 minutes at the end of the afternoon session.

38 hours – weekly, hour-long staff meetings.

162 hours 15 minutes – curriculum responsibilities.

8 hours – attendance at staff/parent consultation evenings.

10 hours 30 minutes – contingency time; to include attendance at PTA meetings
if possible, attendance at school concerts and attendance at any extra staff meetings arranged.

To be reviewed annually.

Appendix 10

Assessing your approach to educational inclusion: two examples

(i) Teaching with Inclusion in Mind: a personal audit

	Rating•	Evidence / Comments
• organisational arrangements	1 2 3 4 5	
• communication	1 2 3 4 5	
• classroom experiences	1 2 3 4 5	
• social climate	1 2 3 4 5	
• relationships	1 2 3 4 5	

* NB. 1 = excellent 2 = good 3 = satisfactory 4 = poor 5 = undeveloped

(ii) Reflecting on my classroom practice

Do I encourage all pupils to take part in all subjects/activities?
Yes   Sometimes   No

COMMENT:

Do I plan lessons with all pupils in mind?
Yes   Sometimes   No

COMMENT:

Do all pupils actually participate during lessons?
Yes   Sometimes   No

COMMENT:

Do I teach using a variety of styles and strategies?
Yes   Sometimes   No

COMMENT:

Do I incorporate opportunities for pupils to arrive at different outcomes?
Yes   Sometimes   No

COMMENT:

Are the children encouraged to evaluate/assess their own learning?
Yes   Sometimes   No

COMMENT:

Do I encourage other adults (especially parents/carers/LSAs) to participate in class?
Yes   Sometimes   No

COMMENT:

Appendix 11(i)

Example of a Learning Support Assistant's job description

JOB DESCRIPTION

Title of Post: Learning Support Assistant

Salary:

Hours: 32.5

Line Manager: SENCO

Responsible to: SENCO, Class teacher

Responsibilities:

In relation to individual students:

- To develop an understanding of the special needs of the students supported.
- To take into account the students' special needs and ensure their access to the lesson and its content through appropriate clarification and explanation.
- To help students record work in an appropriate way.
- To help students develop study and organisational skills.
- To help students keep on task and to build motivation.
- To help reinforce learning.
- To help build the students' confidence and self-esteem.
- To encourage the inclusion of the students within the class.
- To liaise with keyworkers in reviews of IEPs and statements.
- To assist in the development of appropriate resources for students.
- To work with individual students outside the classroom as required.
- To assist in the monitoring of the progress of individual students.

In relation to classroom teachers:

- To support class teachers in the implementation of the students' Individual Education Plans.
- To support and assist class teachers in assessing and evaluating the progress of students with SEN.
- To assist the class teacher in assessing the appropriateness of teaching materials.
- To have regular meetings with teachers to help prepare for and review, lessons.
- Where appropriate, to liaise between student and teacher.
- To provide regular feedback about the child to the teacher.

In relation to the school:

- To work as part of the SEN team.
- To contribute to students' reviews as appropriate.
- To be aware of school policies and procedures, including those relating to confidentiality.
- To identify personal in-service needs and to attend appropriate internal and external in-service training.
- To attend relevant after school meetings.
- To take part in before school and after school activities and supervision of SEN pupils in unstructured times, for periods commensurate with hours worked.
- Any other tasks as directed by the Head Teacher which fall within the purview of the post.

Appendix 11(ii)

Example of an adult helper briefing sheet

Date:	Session focus:

What the children need to do:

What the children need to learn:

Please direct the children's attention by asking questions such as:

Please look out for –
Indicators of success:

Indicators of difficulty:

Feedback on children's learning:

Adapted from © NTU BA (Hons) QTS Year 4. Fourth Teaching Practice Module Handbook 2000/2001

Appendix 12

SEN objectives and action plan for the induction period

Once you have completed training, you should assess what you believe to be your strengths in respect of SEN and then establish a set of priorities for further professional development. This will enable you to prepare for your first teaching post, the induction programme related to it, and your longer term continuing professional development in SEN.

OBJECTIVES	ACTIONS I CAN TAKE	SUCCESS CRITERIA	RESOURCES

Adapted from © NTU BA (Hons) QTS Year 4: Serial Placement Handbook 2000/2001

Appendix 13

Tutors' and Mentors' OHPs

A child has *special educational needs* if he has a *learning difficulty* which calls for *special educational provision* to be made for him.

A child has a *learning difficulty* if he:

(a) has a significantly greater difficulty in learning than the majority of children of the same age; or

(b) has a disability which prevents or hinders the child from making use of educational facilities of a kind generally provided for children of the same age in schools within the area of the local education authority;

(c) is under five and falls within the definition at (a) or (b) above or would do so if special educational provision was not made for the child.

A child must not be regarded as having a learning difficulty solely because the language or medium of communication of the home is different from the language in which he or she is or will be taught.

(Education Act 1996, Section 312)

Mentor/Tutor O/H (1): Definition of SEN

- ## Communication and interaction
- ## Cognition and learning
- ## Behaviour, emotional and social development
- ## Sensory and/or physical

Mentor/Tutor O/H (2): SEN groupings (Code of Practice, 2001)

- ## Pupils who are blind
- ## Pupils who are deaf
- ## Pupils with partial sight
- ## Pupils with partial hearing
- ## Pupils who are termed 'delicate'
- ## Pupils who have speech defects
- ## Pupils who are termed 'maladjusted'
- ## Pupils who have epilepsy
- ## Pupils who are termed 'educationally subnormal'
- ## Pupils who have physical handicap

Mentor/Tutor O/H (3): 'Categories' of handicap (1944 Education Act)

- Working with parents/carers
- Improving the SEN framework
- Developing a more inclusive system
- Developing knowledge and skills
- Working in partnership to meet SENs

Mentor/Tutor O/H (4): 5 core themes of the Programme of Action

- A child with special educational needs should have his needs met
- The special educational needs of children will normally be met in mainstream schools or settings
- The views of the child should be sought and taken into account
- Parents/carers have a vital role to play in supporting their child's education
- Children with special educational needs should be offered full access to a broad, balanced and relevant education, including the Foundation Stage Curriculum and the National Curriculum

Mentor/Tutor O/H (5): Core Principles of the Code of Practice (2001)

- **The culture, practice, management and deployment of resources in school or setting should be designed to ensure all children's needs are met**
- **LEAs, schools and settings should work together to ensure that any child's special educational needs are identified early**
- **LEAs, schools and settings should exploit good and best practice when devising interventions**
- **Those responsible for special educational provision should take into account the wishes of the child concerned, in the light of his age and understanding**
- **Special education professionals work in partnership with parents/carers and take into account the views of individual parents/carers in respect of their child's particular needs**
- **Interventions for each child are reviewed regularly to assess their impact, the child's progress and the views of the child, his teachers and his parents/carers**
- **There is close cooperation between all the agencies concerned and a multi-disciplinary approach to the resolution of issues**

Mentor/Tutor O/H (6): Key factors in meeting special educational needs (Code of Practice, 2001)

Section 1:   **Principles and
               Procedures**

Section 2:   **School-Based Stages
               of Assessment and
               Provision**

Section 3:   **Statutory Assessment
               of SEN**

Section 4:   **Statements of SEN**

Section 5:   **Assessment of Under
               Fives**

Section 6:   **Annual Reviews**

Mentor/Tutor O/H (7): Key areas of activity in the Programme of Action

- **Develop a more inclusive approach to SEN**
- **Achieve better cooperation between education, health and social services**
- **Support for looked-after children**
- **Enhance the role of governing bodies in relation to SEN**
- **Support children aged under five**
- **Enhance the links between Early Years and Sure Start initiatives**
- **Improve the links between exclusions from school and 'education otherwise'**
- **Interface with the National Curriculum and the literacy hour**
- **Enhance the rights of disabled children to personal support**
- **Improve conciliation arrangements**
- **Increase the use of ICT in record keeping**
- **Address the implications for SEN of the National Childcare Strategy and changes to the NHS**
- **Comply with the new school framework and the abolition of the Funding Agency for Schools**

Mentor/Tutor O/H (8): Rationale for changes to the Code of Practice (1994–2001)

- **The child fails to respond to targeted approaches in his area of weakness**
- **The child is slow to develop age-appropriate literacy/numeracy skills**
- **The child presents 'emotional and/or behavioural difficulties' in spite of your use of behaviour management techniques**
- **The child has sensory or physical difficulties and fails to make progress in spite of specialist equipment**
- **The child has communication/interaction difficulties and makes no progress in spite of your differentiated teaching**

Mentor/Tutor O/H (9): triggers for 'School Action'

- **The child continues to fail to respond to targeted approaches in his area of weakness over a long period of time**

- **The child is slow to develop age-appropriate literacy/numeracy skills**

- **The child continues working at National Curriculum levels substantially below that expected of pupils of a similar age**

- **The child presents 'emotional and/or behavioural difficulties' which substantially and regularly interfere with his own learning or that of the class group, in spite of the behaviour management techniques you have attempted**

- **The child has sensory or physical difficulties and requires additional specialist equipment or regular advice or visits from specialist**

- **The child has ongoing communication or interaction difficulties that impede the development of social relationships and cause substantial barriers to learning**

Mentor/Tutor O/H (10): Triggers for 'School Action Plus'

- **The class teacher is responsible for initial identification of a pupil's SEN by (a) observation and (b) continuous assessment**

- **The class teacher must develop differentiated approaches to meet identified needs (ONGOING)**

- **The class teacher MUST inform the SENCO of any concerns which remain, in spite of the initial attempts to meet the pupil's learning needs**

- **The class teacher, working with the SENCO, will decide what help to provide next**

- **The class teacher, working with the SENCO, MUST keep the parents/carers informed and (preferably) invite the parents/carers to discuss the concerns and the action taken (ONGOING)**

Mentor/Tutor O/H (11) Class-teacher responsibilities (Code of Practice, 2001)

- **The class teacher, working with the SENCO, will help devise an IEP – ensuring input from both the parents/carers and the child**

- **The class teacher monitors the progress of the child in meeting IEP targets (ONGOING)**

- **The class teacher arranges and attends review meetings (with SENCO, parent, and where appropriate, the child)**

- **The class teacher MUST inform the SENCO of any continuing concerns (ONGOING)**

- **The class teacher MUST continue to organise and plan her teaching so that the child's needs are met – including directing the work of LSAs and involving the child in his own IEP monitoring (ONGOING)**

Mentor/Tutor O/H (11): Class teacher responsibilities (Code of Practice, 2001)

- **The class teacher MUST continue to support the pupil in the ways described in 'School Action'**
- **The class teacher should utilise any additional resources or advice as specified by external agencies**
- **The class teacher should continue to liaise closely with both SENCO and parents/carers**

Mentor/Tutor O/H (12): The class teacher and 'School Action Plus'

- **Plan your lessons!**
- **Tell your pupils what you want them to achieve by the end of the lesson**
- **Include lots of 'signposts' giving pupils an idea of where the learning is taking them**
- **Offer pupils a range of small tasks with clear learning targets**
- **Keep your instructions clear and short**
- **Mix individual and group work**
- **Use praise consistently**
- **Use differentiation – by input, process and output**
- **Make use of summaries**

Mentor/Tutor O/H (13): Preventing underachievement: some practical solutions

- **Day-to-day management of SEN policy**
- **Liaising with and advising fellow teachers**
- **Coordinating provision for SEN**
- **Maintaining the SEN register and overseeing records**
- **Liaising with parents/carers of children with SEN**
- **Contributing to INSET**
- **Liaising with external agencies**

Mentor/Tutor O/H (14): Initial responsibilities of the SENCO (Code of Practice, 1994)

A. Strategic direction and development of SEN in the school

B. Teaching and Learning

C. Leading and managing staff

D. Efficient/effective deployment of staff/resources

Mentor/Tutor O/H (15): Key areas of SENCO responsibility (National Standards for SENCOS)

- Overseeing the day-to-day operation of the school's SEN policy
- Coordinating provision for children with SEN
- Liaising with and advising fellow teachers
- managing LSAs
- Overseeing the records on all children with SEN
- Liaising with parents/carers of children with SEN
- Contributing to the in-service training of staff
- liaising with external agencies

Mentor/Tutor O/H (16); SENCO responsibilities under the Code of Practice, (2001)

- **Be seen as a working document**
- **Use a simple format**
- **Specify ONLY additional targets**
- **Avoid jargon**
- **Be comprehensible to staff and parents/carers**
- **Be distributed to all staff**
- **Promote effective planning**
- **Help pupils understand own progress**
- **Result in action/specific learning goals**

Mentor/Tutor O/H (17): Key characteristics of effective IEPs

Subject Index

able pupils 19, 122
abuse 90
admission arrangements 23, 56, 57, 118
adviser/inspector 79, 123
advocacy 77, 88, 90
annual report 70, 107, 110, 119
Asperger's Syndrome 20
assessment 12, 21, 22, 27, 29, 33, 35–9, 41,
    42, 56, 57, 63, 64, 74, 75, 78, 84, 105–8,
    119–22, 125, 128
attendance 27, 75, 80
Attention Deficit Hyperactivity Disorder
    (ADHD) 90,
attention span 27
Autistic Spectrum Disorder (ASD) 14, 20,
    80, 88, 90, 109

barriers to learning 7, 37, 64, 75, 76
behaviour 8, 19, 20, 27, 41, 44, 66–73, 89,
    90, 97, 111, 112
behaviour/discipline policy 23, 66, 69, 72,
    75, 123
behaviour management 21, 23, 36, 37, 62,
    66, 69, 71, 81, 82, 88
behaviour support plan 23
blind 11
bullying 27, 75

categories 9, 11, 13, 67, 88, 89, 95, 105
child protection 79, 90
Children Act 76, 90, 104
circular 6/94 55, 57, 104
circular 8/94 69, 70, 104
circular 9/94 69, 104
classroom organisation 28, 31, 70, 81, 82, 114
code of conduct 69
Code of Practice 2, 3, 4, 7, 8, 18–24, 25, 27,
    33–7, 39, 40, 41, 47, 48, 51, 52, 55, 56, 57,

62, 75, 76, 77, 84, 85, 97, 104, 106, 107,
    110, 118, 119
cognition 8, 20, 27, 44
cognitive impairment/delay 19, 68, 80
collaboration 23, 24, 29, 52, 62, 69, 71, 74,
    75, 78, 81, 82, 85
communication 7, 8, 19, 27, 31, 36, 37, 43,
    44, 48, 70, 83, 86, 125
community 74, 76
concept map 30, 31
conciliation 34
confidence 63, 68, 128
confidentiality 82, 128
connexions 80, 104
consultant 37, 38
continuum 12, 26
co-ordination 34, 44, 47, 48, 56, 75, 90, 106,
    107, 108, 118, 119, 121
counselling 20, 53
cultural development 63
curriculum 19–23, 30, 38, 43, 44, 48, 52, 56,
    57, 60–5, 81, 89, 106, 107, 112, 122, 124,
    125

deaf 11, 20
delicate 11
diagnostic 74, 120
differentiation 31, 36, 42, 46, 60–63, 65, 70,
    81, 106
disability 14, 15
disaffection 67, 69
disapplication 60, 120, 122
discipline 67, 69, 70, 75, 124
disruptive behaviour 12, 16, 20, 67, 68
Down's Syndrome 14
drugs 88, 89
dyslexia 19, 20
dyspraxia 74, 120

Author Index